T0103936

A GUIDE TO PRACTICAL LIVING

Insights from the Epistle of James

WILLIAM GOLSON JR.

Order this book online at www.trafford.com
or email orders@trafford.com

Most Trafford titles are also available at major online book retailers.

Print information available on the last page.

ISBN: 978-1-4907-6659-1 (sc)
ISBN: 978-1-4907-6658-4 (e)

Trafford rev. 11/03/2015

www.trafford.com

North America & international
toll-free: 1 888 232 4444 (USA & Canada)
fax: 812 355 4082

CONTENTS

ACKNOWLEDGEMENTS

It has been my privilege for more than 27 years to pastor and preach to the membership of True Light Baptist Church. During this time as I have prayerfully attempted to address their needs, God has faithfully spoken into my life as well. I have grown in wisdom and benefited through the opportunity to address relevant issues biblically. This compilation of sermons is influenced by the circumstances, situations, and opportunities of those who have allowed me to share in resolution of their challenges.

My deepest thank goes out to those who have contributed in their own way to the context of this work, my loving and supportive congregation, and those who have allowed me to be a part of providing counsel in their lives. I am thankful to have been a part of their lives. *"Ointment and perfume delight the heart, and the sweetness of a man's friend gives delight by hearty counsel."* (Proverbs 27:9)

Thanks to my staff (Sable Golson, Bonne Tootle, and Jeanie Draper) who diligently ensure that I have the time to do what is needful and are always willing to do whatever it takes to make their pastor "look good."

I dedicate this work to my dear mother who went home to be with the Lord (June 2015). Whatever I have become is a result of having come from good seed, and having been nurtured along the way by a true example of a saintly mother. Her wisdom, example of righteous living, and love for the Lord have been and will continue to be my guide and strength. My parents, William and Maldoshia, were married for over 68 years and gave their full support for my ministry.

In addition, I dedicate it to my wife, Melvia Jo who has helped me to understand the meaning of being a husband and father and allowing me to be her pastor. Thanks to my children Melody and William III, who have endured, in the arena of raising them to adulthood, my often-misguided attempts at parenting, but who in spite of my mistakes, by God's grace; have grown to be godly individuals of whom I proudly boast to be my children. *"Behold, children are a heritage from the Lord, the fruit of the womb is a reward. Like arrows in the hand of a warrior, so are the children of one's youth. Happy is the man who has his quiver full of them; they shall not be ashamed, but shall speak with their enemies in the gate"* (Psalm 127:3-5). Thank you.

INTRODUCTION

The Epistle of James is the "how-to" book of the Christian life. It is one of the most practical books in the New Testament because it offers instruction and exhortation to Christians who are experiencing problems. Additionally, it was written to help us understand what it means to mature as Christians. Though not universally agreed upon, the evidence is strong that James is one of the oldest books in the New Testament.

All believers need to have as a goal to achieve spiritual maturity. As we read the epistle, we discover that these Jewish Christians were having some problems in their personal lives and in their church fellowship. They were going through difficult testings'. They were also facing temptations to sin. Some of the believers were catering to the rich, while the rich were robbing others. Church members were competing for offices in the church, particularly teaching offices. One of the major problems in the church was a failure of many to live what they professed to believe. Furthermore, the tongue was a serious problem, even to the point of creating wars and divisions in the assembly. Worldliness was another problem. Some of the members were sick physically because they were disobeying God's Word, and some were straying away from the Lord and the church.

As we review this list of problems, do they appear to be much different from the problems that beset the average local church today? Is not worldliness a serious problem? Are there not Christians who cannot control their tongues? It seems that James is dealing with very up to-date matters. He was not discussing an array of miscellaneous problems; all of these problems had a common cause—a lack of spiritual maturity. These Christians were simply not growing up.

Spiritual maturity is also one of the greatest needs in churches today. Too many churches are playpens for babies, instead of workshops for adults. The members are not mature enough to eat the solid food that they need, so they have to be fed milk. God is looking for mature men and women to carry on his work, and sometimes all he can find are little children who cannot even get along with each other. If Christians would just grow up, they would become victors instead of victims.

James is a common name in the New Testament. The accompanying phrase could have described any Christian, suggesting that this particular James must have been a church leader who needed no further introduction. Four men named "James" are mentioned in the New Testament:

- James, the son of Zebedee and brother of John (Matt. 4:21), a disciple and apostle of Christ
- James, the son of Alphaeus (Matt. 10:3), called "the Less" or "the Younger," also one of the apostles
- James, the father of an apostle named Judas (Luke 6:16)
- James, the half-brother of Jesus, traditionally called "the Just" (Matt. 13:55)

James the Just was the leader of the Jerusalem church (Acts 15:3; Gal. 2:9) and seems to be the most probable author of this epistle. If he was the author, it is noteworthy that he did not mention his relation to Jesus in this letter.

Some believe this letter was directed to all Jews living outside of Palestine, including both Christian and non-Christian Jews. This seems unlikely; however, since James identifies himself as a follower of Christ and refers to his readers as a community of believers (1:18; 2:1, 7; 5:7). Others hold that the salutation is a figurative reference to all Christian churches, represented symbolically by ancient Israel. This too is improbable since the letter contains recognizable Jewish elements. There is also a third possibility, that the readers were Jewish Christians living outside of Palestine. Since this letter was, a circular letter that was passed from church to church, no specific geographical destination is pinpointed. Most of the recipients seem to have been poor and suffering from oppression imposed by their fellow Jews, among whom they were living. Evidently, some of these Jewish Christians had been imprisoned and deprived of their possessions and livelihoods. Under such conditions, they fell into the clutches of worldliness, fought among themselves, favored the rich over the poor, and lost their original love for one another.

James says little about Jesus. He begins his book referring to the Lord Jesus Christ (1:1; 2:1) and anticipates "the coming of the Lord" (5:7), but that is about it in terms of direct references. Still, James' message is virtually saturated in Jesus' teachings (Matthew 5, 6).

The major theological issue in James is faith and works (2:14–26). James is not questioning whether the recipients were genuine believers; he repeatedly calls them "brethren," "my brethren," or "my beloved brethren" (2:1, 14). Clearly, these people were exercising saving faith. Thus, what James is discussing is faith that is alone, meaning without works. He calls faith without works "dead," indicating that it was faith that was once alive (2:17, 26). For James, works is a natural result of faith. When a person truly believes in something, he or she will act on that belief. With this letter, James was sounding a wake-up call to all Christians: "Get your life in line with what you believe!"

Contrary to what we might think, not everyone who grows old grows up. There is a difference between age and maturity. Just because a Christian has been saved for 10 or 20 years does not guarantee that they are mature in the Lord. Christian growth is not automatic, as is physical growth. Ideally, the older we are, the more mature we should be; but too often, the ideal does not become the reality. Christian maturity is something we must work at constantly. We must make a concerted effort to achieve an understanding of the truths of God's Word. Mature Christians are happy Christians, useful Christians, and Christians who help to encourage others and to build their local church. As we study James together, my hope and my prayer is that we will, with God's help, learn together and mature together.

CHAPTER 1

"LET'S MEET THE MAN"

"James, a bondservant of God and of the Lord Jesus Christ, to the twelve tribes which are scattered abroad: Greetings." (James 1:1)

Apostolic letters, that is, those written by those who were with Jesus from the beginning and who were witnesses of the risen Christ (Acts 1:21, 22) constitute 21 of the 27 books of the New Testament.

James is one of the few books in the New Testament that was not written by an apostle. By nearly all accounts, this was the first book written in the New Testament. It was probably written between 44 and 49 AD, just a handful of years after the death, burial, and resurrection of our Lord.

The Book of James, as we will see, is incredibly practical. The book addresses many issues that are relevant to life in today's society. It addresses such issues as authenticity in our faith, temptation, anger, gossip, favoritism, procrastination, dealing with wealth, church leadership, and the list goes on.

James gets immediately to the subject at hand. James defines his spiritual relationship to the Lord Jesus Christ and addresses the Jewish believers dispersed at large.

WHO IS THIS JAMES?

"James . . ." (vs. 1a)

As was the custom with letter writing some two thousand years ago, the author of this book, or letter, identified himself at the beginning instead of the end, as we see in letter writing today. However, who was this James who wrote the letter we are looking at? Over the centuries, there have been several theories as to the identity of the author.

James was a common name in New Testament times. This James must therefore have occupied a position of prominence in the early Christian movement, which the use of a single name would distinguish him as it did with the apostle Paul from others with this name. James was assured the readers would know him.

There are names that we immediately recognize with prominent personalities: in the political arena—John F, Barak, Martin, Jessie; in sports—Magic, Kobe, LeBron; and in music—JayZ, Beyoncé, Quincy. At the mention of their name most of us know who they are.

The world knows us by our name. It tells our history—our reputation. Sometimes it can be hard to live up to our name. Sometimes it can be hard to live our name down. However, even though our name ties us to our family name, it speaks even louder of our own reputation. James was that way. His name spoke of his identity in the world.

In the New Testament world James was not an uncommon name, as it is today. In simply stating his name, it is evident that knowledge of him, and who he was, would have been readily accepted and understood.

Four men named James are recorded in the New Testament. The first is James the son of Zebedee and brother of the Apostle John. He was the first apostle to suffer martyrdom being killed by Herod Agrippa around 44 AD (Acts 12:1, 2). The second James was the father of the Apostle Judas (not Iscariot) (Luke 6:16, Acts 1:13). Nothing is known of him. The third was James the son of Alphaeus, also one of the Apostles (Luke 6:15) and is usually identified as James the less (Mark 15:40). His name-drops out of the apostolic record with those mentioned. Finally, there was James the half-brother of our Lord. Matthew 13:55 and Mark 6:3 records that Jesus had at least four brothers, *"James, Joses, Simon, and Judas."* James was the second son of Mary, the first son of Joseph and Mary. Tradition has assigned this letter to the brother of Jesus. Others would have died or dropped out of sight.

James exercised great influence among Jewish believers. Acts 12:17 records that there was a James who had a leadership role in the church. He seems to have been head of the Jerusalem Congregation from 48-62 AD and before that time, he was one of its early pillars. Peter after having been released by angels from prison tells those who had been praying for him *"how the Lord had brought him out of the prison. And he said, "Go, tell these things to James and to the brethren." And he departed and went to another place.* Though he is not one of the original 12 apostles, Paul calls him an apostle in Galatians 1:19, *But I saw none of the other apostles except James, the Lord's brother.*

He was recognized as the first bishop of Jerusalem and was given the title *'James the Just'* because of his righteousness and faithfulness to the law and the early church called him "old camel knees" because of his incredible prayer life. The scribes and Pharisees stoned James for refusing to renounce his commitment to Jesus in 62 AD.

JAMES RELATIONSHIP TO JESUS.

> *". . . a bondservant of God and of the Lord Jesus Christ* (vs. 1b)

Although "the Lord's brother" and the recognized leader of the Jerusalem church, James shows his true humility of spirit by calling himself *simply "a bondservant of God and of the Lord Jesus Christ."*

Jewish Christians to whom James was writing to understood what he meant by the term 'bondservant'. A bondservant was one who was in essence a slave. According to Deuteronomy 15:12-17 and under Old Testament Law, a servant was to be freed during the Jubilee year (every 50 years). That passage of the Law required the Jews to set their slaves free after six years of service. However, a servant could by choice refuse freedom and become part of the household. If the slave loved his master, he could choose to stay forever. If he freely chose to do so, he would be taken to the doorpost of the house and his ear would be pierced with an awl. This choice was made out of a sense of love and loyalty.

I believe James may have been referencing this choice. He was (by choice) a servant of Christ. He humbled himself to this position and it was the perfect position to use to present the truths he was about to share in this letter. He did not assert authority even though he spoke with authority.

In stating himself to be *a bondservant of God and of the Lord Jesus Christ*, James places Christ on the same plane with the God of the Old Covenant. This is a powerful confession for one with whom he shared a home in Nazareth, and boyhood memories of playing in the Galilean hills. Yet, James confesses that his brother is now his Lord and deserves equal devotion with God.

If we were to reflect on James earlier life, it seems that he did not believe in Jesus during our Lord's lifetime. John 7:5 makes it very clear that James and his brothers were skeptical of Jesus, *for even His brothers did not believe in Him.* They refused to believe that their brother, Jesus, was the Son of God and the Savior of the world. It appears that James was converted soon after the Resurrection.

Those who are our relations, who grow up and live with us, know us the best. It is said that you never really know someone until you live with him or her. Some of you, who had friends that turned into roommates, were highly disappointed after living with them, and you know what I mean.

Some of us have relatives and relations who say that they are called to ministry. Having lived with them, and observed them up close, we find it hard to believe. Can you imagine the difficulty of growing up with a brother and now having to believe he is supposedly the Son of God?

So when did James give his life to Christ? There is no mention of James' salvation in any of the four gospel stories. James and his brothers were spiritually dead in their unbelief. However, having witnessed the crucifixion, and the resurrection, at least one of the brothers, James, is converted. James acknowledged Jesus Christ as more than his older brother who died on the cross.

In Jesus post-resurrection appearance, we read in 1 Corinthians 15:6, 7 that James, the brother of Jesus, was not a follower until after the resurrection. In his post-resurrection appearance, Jesus we are told, he "*. . . was seen by over five hundred brethren at once, of whom the greater part remain to the present, but some have fallen asleep. After that He was seen by James, then by all the apostles.*" James became a Christian when we saw the risen Jesus (1 Corinthians 15:7) and went on to become a leader in the church at Jerusalem (Acts 12:17; 15:13ff; 21:18).

Somewhere during one of these post-resurrection appearances, James bowed his knee to Jesus, acknowledging Him as his Lord and Savior. James recognized that his real relationship to Jesus was not physical, but spiritual, made possible by the grace of God alone.

James was a new man.

- Resentment was replaced by repentance
- Antagonism was replaced by adoration
- Prejudice was replaced by praise and thanksgiving
- The Holy Spirit moved in James' heart
- The veil was lifted from James' eyes

The truth according to man was replaced with the truth according to God the Father, through His Son Jesus Christ. James now saw Jesus as the Way, and the Truth, and the Life. He no longer looked at Jesus as the older brother who was too good to be true. His skepticism was replaced by salvation.

James, known as "James the Just" by his Jewish contemporaries, never used his pedigree as the half-brother of

Jesus as a means to prominence or notoriety. One ancient historian recorded that James, "used to enter alone into the temple and be found kneeling and praying for forgiveness for the people, so that his knees grew hard like a camel's because of his constant worship of God. So, from his excessive righteousness he was called the Just." [1] He did not use his position as brother to Jesus as a privilege. In spite of all his position and authority, James modestly refers to himself as the bondservant, or slave, of his illustrious Brother and of God.

TO WHOM WAS THIS LETTER WRITTEN?

> *". . . to the twelve tribes which are scattered abroad: Greetings."* (vs. 1c)

This letter was written from Jerusalem, where, by this time, James was serving as one of the leaders of the church. The majority of believers at the time were Jewish by birth and the gospel had not yet reached much of the Gentile world. "The twelve tribes" was a common reference to the nation of Israel. Israel's historical twelve tribes no longer existed in a physical sense. The term became a popular way of describing the gathered and spiritually renewed Israel that would be brought into being in the last days. Given this background, James may have chosen the designation "twelve tribes" in order to signify his intention to address the Jewish people as a whole, non-Christians, as well as Christians. [2]

As for those "scattered abroad," this is thought to be a reference to those, the true Israel, living outside Palestine (Jerusalem) whose home is heaven and whose present state is that of 'strangers and pilgrims' upon this earth (Hebrews 11:13; 13:14). In this sense, it

---

1 http://*www.sermoncentral.com/And* to Think I Called Him Crazy by Tom Miano

2 Douglas J. Moo, *The Letter of James* (Grand Rapids, MI: William B. Eerdmans, 2000), 31.

is addressed to all of Christian character and content, as heaven is our home.

The attractive suggestion that Acts 11:19 may provide the specific background for James use of *scattered.* Here Luke tells us that, as result of the persecution connected with the stoning of Stephen, many Jewish Christians were scattered. The Greek word for scattered is used in the sense of broadcasting seed over an open field.

Acts 11:19-21 tells us, *"Now those who were scattered after the persecution that arose over Stephen traveled as far as Phoenicia, Cyprus, and Antioch, preaching the word to no one but the Jews only. But some of them were men from Cyprus and Cyrene, who, when they had come to Antioch, spoke to the Hellenists, preaching the Lord Jesus. And the hand of the Lord was with them, and a great number believed and turned to the Lord."*

Unlike the Pauline epistles that are written towards specific churches in specific cities: Romans, Corinth, Galatia, Philippi, and Ephesus; James is the first in a group of letters addressed to Christians in general. It is an extremely practical letter about the Christian life.

James is a more general letter. He is writing to the problem that a type of believer might experience wherever they may be. James was written not to one particular congregation, but overall to congregations that were scattered throughout the known world. James writes his letter, establishing a measuring stick for true spiritual maturity.

James wrote to help Christians and churches obtain spiritual maturity. Spiritual maturity is still one of the greatest needs in churches today. Too many churches are playpens for baby Christians instead of workshops for the mature. The members are not grown enough to eat the solid spiritual food so they need to be maintained on milk. God is looking for mature men and women to carry on His great enterprise of redemption but often finding only children who have not even learned how to get along with one another. [3]

****

In order to attain Christian maturity and holy conduct it is essential to have a firm foundation. As believers, we must be able to stand with confidence. We must not be beaten down by trials nor fall by temptation. How can such stamina be achieved? This study of James will prepare us to withstand trials from without and temptations from within and become a Christian who can stand in truth.

James received salvation almost two thousand years ago the same way people come to a personal relationship with Jesus Christ today. Our society, the world we live in, is much different from the world that James lived in. However, the truth of God's word remains the same. The way to eternal life remains the same. Jesus Christ is still changing lives today the way he did for His younger brother all those years ago. Nothing is more relevant to our lives than our need for a Savior. Nothing is more relevant to our lives than where we will spend eternity.

The awesome thing is that the gift of salvation, by the grace of God afforded to James, is available to anyone who will call on the name of Jesus Christ and ask Him to be his or her Lord and Savior.

Have you experienced the truth of the Gospel? If not we invite you to come and get to know James' half-brother just as James did. James decision was that Jesus is Lord and that he would serve Him as His bondservant. What is yours?

REFLECTIONS AND MEDITATIONS

1. What bearing does your name have on the influence, or lack thereof, of those who know you?

---

3 http://www.sermoncentral.com/sermon/The Writer and Readers of James by Dennis Davidson

2. What convinced or convicted you that Jesus was more than just a historical figure, that, he was and is the Son of God.
3. How would you rate your level of spiritual maturity?

CHAPTER 2

"THE TESTING OF FAITH"

James 1:1-12

> During times when the love and grace of God seem to be overshadowed by trials and tribulations we can find light, we can find strength, to endure by understanding the reason behind our circumstances.

> *"My brethren, count it all joy when you fall into various trials." (James 1:2)*

Without a doubt if there has not already been there will be a season, there will inevitably be a time, when it will seem as if the sun has set in your life. There will be times when each of us will experience some darkness. No matter how well we live, we will feel all alone sometimes. There will be times when we feel tempted and tried by circumstances that will disappoint us, disadvantage us, discourage us, and make us feel estranged from God. When instead of basking in the sunshine of God's grace, we find ourselves confused trying to find our way. How do we handle days when our faith is tested? How we handle days when we are beset with difficulties; when the ball is in our court; when it rains on our parade? How do you handle days when trouble knocks at the front door and trials at the back? Where do we find strength?

Let us consider; if we want to have a positive testimony of faith, if we are going to turn trials into triumphs, pains into praise, grief into glory, and problems into power . . .

WE MUST HAVE A JOYFUL RESPONSE TO TROUBLE IN OUR LIVES.

> *"My brethren, count it all joy when you fall into various trials"* (vs. 2)

In the realm of human response, at face value, this would appear to be a contradiction of terms that joy and trials, or what the KJV translates temptations, should be so related. This would seem to be inconsistent with the reality of life. We usually connect the word joy with delight, not trials, or temptations. How many people do you know that anticipate and endure problems in their life with joy? God tells us through James to expect trials. It is not "if you fall into various trials "but *"when you fall into various trials."* The believer who expects their Christian life to be easy is in for a shock. The fact of the matter is that we will have some trials in our lives just by living. Why? Because. . .

- We are imperfect beings, dwelling in imperfect bodies
- We eat imperfect food, grown in an imperfect world, processed by imperfect people
- We have imperfect relationships with imperfect family, and imperfect friends
- We work on imperfect jobs, with imperfect people
- We set imperfect goals, and we use imperfect means to attain them
- Our whole existence is imperfect

Since the original sin of Adam and Eve in the Garden of Eden, people have been imperfect beings victimized by sin. Romans 3:23

tells us, *"For all have sinned and fall short of the glory of God."* The only sinless human being was Christ; he was perfect. However, even Jesus was tempted, even Jesus was subjected to difficulties. Even though he was perfect, he had to deal with imperfect people, in an imperfect world.

The point is this. If we continue to live, we are going to have some problems in our lives. The imperfections of the world dictate that not all will be perfect.

- We are going to have some sickness
- We are going to have some conflicts with family, friends, and loved ones
- We are going to be disappointed in those whom we put confidence
- We are going to have troubles on our job

Yes, the evidence that we are imperfect should lead us to expect calamity, confrontations, physical, mental, and spiritual trials. Yes, there will be some trying times in our lives. Days when our faith is tested. We cannot expect everything to go our way. Some trials come simply because we are human. Other trials come because we are Christians. Peter emphasizes this in his first letter: *"Beloved, do not think it strange concerning the fiery trial which is to try you, as though some strange thing happened to you"* (1 Peter 4:12). Satan fights us, the world opposes us, and this makes for a lifelong battle.

Nevertheless, we need not dwell in the valley of despair. We need not settle for every trial that awaits us. In all our problems, we can have joy, we can rejoice. We can look beyond the trials and see what is on the other side. We can look for the positive beyond the negative. How? The key word is "*count*." It is a financial term, and it means to "evaluate." When we face the trials of life, we must evaluate them in the light of what God is doing to us and for us. Our values determine our evaluations.

- If we value comfort more than character, then trials will upset us.

- If we value the material and physical more than the spiritual, we will not be able to "*count it all joy.*"
- If we live only for the present and forget the future, then trials will make us bitter and not better.

A carpenter who was hired to help restore an old farmhouse had just finished a rough first day on the job. A flat tire had made him lose an hour of work, his electric saw quit, and now his ancient pickup refused to start.

As the man who had hired him drove him home, he sat in stony silence. On arriving, he invited the man in to meet his family. As they walked toward the front door, he paused briefly at a small tree, touching the tips of the branches with both hands. Then opening the door, he underwent an amazing transformation. His face was covered in smiles and he hugged his two small children and gave his wife a kiss.

Afterwards the carpenter walked the man to the car. They passed the tree, and the man's curiosity got the better of him. He asked him about what he had done earlier. "Oh, that is my trouble tree," he replied. "I know I can't help having them on the job, but one thing is for sure—troubles don't belong in the house with my wife and the children. Therefore, I just hang them on the tree every night when I come home. Then in the morning, I pick them up again. "Funny thing is," he said smilingly, "When I come out in the morning to pick them up, there aren't nearly as many as I remember hanging up the night before." We need to hang our problems on God's tree.[4]

WE MUST UNDERSTAND GOD'S METHOD FOR SPIRITUAL PROGRESSION.

> *"Knowing that the testing of your faith produces patience. But let patience have its perfect work, that*

---

[4] http://www.sermoncentral.com/Illustrations/The Trouble Tree/sermon-illustration-stories-parenting-disappointment-guilt-8631.asp

> *you may be perfect and complete, lacking nothing."* (vs. 3-4)

Looking at these verses carefully, we observe two things. First, testing or troubles are not to be taken as personal offences. James says, *"Knowing that the testing of your faith produces patience."* Faith is the target, not us. God directs specific tests our way to stretch us spiritually, to move us from where we are to where we need to be.

Some of us walk in the sunshine more than others do. Generally, there are periods in time when we are basking in the sunshine of God's grace and mercy. These are followed by periods when things are dim or dark.

- When it seems as if our prayers are unanswered
- When sometimes we don't even know what to pray for
- Times when it seems as if God is calling us to a great work but won't tell us what it is, or how to go about it
- Times when it seems that Satan bombards us with every temptation at his disposal

In addition, we cry out in the darkness of our circumstance wishing, hoping, and praying that God will give us some direct light: that he would make his will evident, that there would be some kind of direct communication, and that someone used of God would come and relay his will to us, but it does not happen.

It is during those times that we have to rely upon our own internal source of light. Christians have sort of an internal spiritual battery pack that is charged by the Spirit of God during good days, when troubles are few. During the day, when we can see clearly, we need to charge our spiritual battery: When things are going well, when our health is good, when financially we are prospering. We need to charge our spiritual batteries during good days for when trials and tribulations come in like a flood; when it seems that no one is for us and all are against us; when it seems that God for a season has no answers in his out basket of prayer, then we can turn on our own spiritual light and we can go on for a while illuminated by the light of faith through the Holy Spirit.

In the context of spiritual progress each period of light is seemingly followed by a period of dark when God allows us

- To reason in our own mind
- To contemplate in our own heart
- To utilize what we have stored away during the day
- To exercise the faith, the belief, and the trust that we claim to have

God allows us to do some spiritual aerobics that our hearts might be made stronger, our hearts might be fixed and our minds made up; that through it all, we might learn patience, and we might learn to endure, that we might come to truly believe and act on the promises of God.

If we understand God's method of spiritual progression, we see that light is followed by darkness by light at a higher plateau, by dark by light at a higher plateau. We spiritually work our way up the ladder of faith. Each rung, each trial, takes us higher and higher in our quest for spiritual maturity. There is no substitute for an understanding mind. Satan can defeat the ignorant believer, but he cannot overcome the Christian who knows the Bible and understands the purposes of God.

Second, God wants us to learn endurance. James 1:4 declares, *"But let patience have its perfect work, that you may be perfect and complete, lacking nothing."* The word endurance literally means to abide under, to be patient. God allows his servants to be tested to bring into our lives those circumstances that can teach us something of significance. The ultimate object of God in allowing us to be tested is to help us reach spiritual maturity. To get us to the point that we not only claim the promises of God, but appropriate and practice them in everyday real life situations.

In the Bible, patience is not a passive acceptance of circumstances. It is a courageous perseverance in the face of suffering and difficulty. Immature people are always impatient;

mature people are patient and persistent. Impatience and unbelief usually go together, just as faith and patience do.

God wants to make us patient because that is the key to every other blessing. The little child who does not learn patience will not learn much of anything else. When we learn to wait on the Lord, then God can do great things for us. God must work in us before he can work through us.

- God spent 245 years working in Abraham before he could give him his promised son.
- God worked 13 years in Joseph's life, putting him into "various testings" before he could put him on the throne of Egypt.
- He spent 80 years preparing Moses for 40 years of leading the children of Israel in the wilderness
- Our Lord Jesus Christ took three years training His disciples, building their character, for continued ministry following his death.

One way the Lord can develop patience and character in our lives is through trials. Reading a book, listening to a sermon, or even praying a prayer cannot attain endurance. Testing burns off excess baggage and inappropriate priorities. It often helps us to see where our real values lie. We must go through the difficulties of life, trust God, and obey him. The result will be patience and character. Knowing this, we can face trails joyfully.

When patience has had its perfect work, when we have learned the lesson that God wants us to learn, when we have moved to the position to which God wants us, we once again dwell in the light but at a higher spiritual plateau.

WE MUST HAVE A HEART THAT WANTS TO BELIEVE.

> *"If any of you lacks wisdom, let him ask of God, who gives to all liberally and without reproach, and it will be given to him. But let him ask in faith, with no*

> *doubting, for he who doubts is like a wave of the sea driven and tossed by the wind. For let not that man suppose that he will receive anything from the Lord; he is a double-minded man, unstable in all his ways."* (vs. 5-8)

What should we pray about when we are going through God-ordained difficulties? James gives the answer. James says that, *"If any of you lacks wisdom, let him ask of God."*

Someone has said that knowledge is the ability to take things apart, while wisdom is the ability to put them together. Wisdom is the right use of knowledge. A person may know a great deal, and yet not be a wise person. All of us know people who have brilliant academic records, but they cannot make the simplest decisions in life. Wisdom shows itself not so much in doing the right thing, as in doing it at the proper time. It proposes right ends, and chooses the best means by which to reach them.

Why do we need wisdom when we are going through trials? Why not ask for strength, grace, or even deliverance. For this reason, we need wisdom so we will not waste the opportunities God is giving us to mature. Wisdom helps us understand how to use these circumstances for our good and God's glory.

How are we to receive wisdom? James says, *"Let him ask of God . . . and it will be given to him."* It interesting that we are not told to read the Bible, or to go to college, or study, but to ask God for this kind of wisdom. Moreover, if you ask for wisdom James says that God *"gives to all liberally and without reproach."* When Solomon asked only for wisdom, God gave him riches and honor too. It is his way *"to do exceedingly abundantly above all that we ask or think"* (Ephesians 3:20). The Lord always gives liberally, never with a grudge, and never ungraciously. God scolds no one for their great ignorance, or for their enormous guilt, or for making himself a last resort, or for coming too often, or for asking too much. We have only to ask, and it shall be given us.

James not only explained what to ask for, wisdom, but he also described how to ask. We are to ask in faith, for God is eager to answer, and he will never scold us. The greatest enemy to answered prayer is unbelief. Prayer is not real unless it is the expression of faith. In the case of many Christians, an imperfect faith in God's readiness to respond to their prayers is one of the greatest defects of their spiritual life. Nothing doubting should be the Christian motto. We cannot petition and shift backwards and forwards between faith and doubt, like a tumbling billow of the sea. We must now swing like a pendulum between cheerful confidence and dark suspicion. Our fixed persuasion must be that God is, and that he does hear and answer prayer.

We should not pray so much for the removal of an affliction as for wisdom to make the right use of it. To be wise in trying times is a special gift of God, and to him we must pray for it.

****

A young boy carried the cocoon of a moth into his house to watch a fascinating event that would take place when the moth emerged. When the moth finally started to break out of his cocoon, the boy noticed how very hard the moth had to struggle. The process was very slow. In an effort to help, he reached down and widened the opening of the cocoon. Soon the moth emerged out of its prison. As the boy watched, the wings remained shriveled. Something was wrong. What the boy had not realized was that the struggle to get out of the cocoon was essential of the moth's muscle system to develop. In an effort to relieve a struggle, the boy had crippled the future of the creature.

In order for us to view our trials with the proper mindset, we have to comprehend their result. We need to realize that as hard as they may be, physically, emotionally, and spiritually they are not bad for us. Without them, we would never develop our spiritual muscles. First, we must endure the cross, then the crown; first the suffering, then the glory. God does not help us by removing the tests, but by making the tests work for us. Satan wants to use the tests to tear us down, but God uses them to build us up.

Perhaps you have seen the bumper sticker that reads, "When life hands you a lemon, make lemonade." What James is trying to tell us is that if you understand what God is trying to do:

- You can turn life's lemons into lemonade
- You can find light in the midst of darkness
- You can find joy in trouble
- Victory in defeat
- Winning in losing
- Uplifting in being downtrodden

During times when the love and grace of God seems to be overshadowed by trials and tribulations, when it seems every element of your faith is being tested; we can find strength, to endure by seeking to understand the reason behind our circumstances and recognize that God has reason and purpose in everything he does.

REFLECTIONS AND MEDITATIONS

1. What do you do with problems that are overwhelming and threaten to consume you?
2. As you reflect upon various trials and testings' you have been through, can you recognize spiritual growth and maturity?
3. In what ways has your faith in God been strengthened as you have seen the positive results of the trials and tests you have endured?

CHAPTER 3

"THE EASY WAY OUT"

James 1:13-18

We cannot blame God for sin resultant of our choices in response to our lustful desire.

> *"But each one is tempted when he is drawn away by his own desires and enticed." (James 1:14)*

A man by the name of J. Wilbur Chapman said, "Temptation is the tempter looking through the keyhole into the room where you are living; sin is you unlocking the door and making it possible for him to enter in."

We are all tempted, and if we do not understand who the author of temptation is, and how temptation leads to sin we can unknowingly unlock the door and let sin in. If we are not careful, we can allow the temptations on the outside to come in, set up residence on the inside, being *"drawn away by his own desires and enticed"* (James 1:14).

A temptation is an opportunity to accomplish a good thing, or to obtain something, in a bad way, apart from the will of God. When circumstances and situations are difficult, we may find ourselves complaining against God, questioning His love, and resisting His will. At this point, Satan provides us with an opportunity to escape the difficulty. This opportunity is a temptation. Satan provides us with an opportunity to take "the easy way out."

Is it wrong to want to pass an examination? Of course not; but if we cheat to pass it, then we have sinned. We have taken "the easy way out." The temptation to cheat is an opportunity to accomplish a good thing (passing the examination) in a bad way. It is not wrong to eat; but if we consider stealing the food, we are tempting ourselves and placing ourselves in a position to sin. Certainly, God does not want us to yield to temptation. He does not want us to take "the easy way out," yet neither can He spare us the experience of temptation. However, if we are mature, we can face testing and temptations with victory. We need not succumb to Satan's opportunity to take "the easy way out." We need not yield to the desire to accomplish a good thing in a bad way, out of the will of God. We need not open the door and let sin in.

James presents three basic facts regarding temptation that we must understand and accept before we can ever begin to deal with the problem itself. Let us consider these facts.

TEMPTATION IS ALWAYS PRESENT IN LIFE, BUT IS NEVER PROMPTED BY GOD.

> *"Let no one say when he is tempted, "I am tempted by God"; for God cannot be tempted by evil, nor does He Himself tempt anyone."* (vs. 13)

James declares, not if, but when we are tempted! Temptation is inevitable. On earth, we will never know a place where our flesh will not be aroused in some way towards wrong things. There will be few times where our minds will dwell on nothing but pure and wholesome thoughts.

James' usage of the word tempt has the idea of Satan's soliciting, or enticing us to do evil. This is in contrast to the testing God might allow. God tests us to stretch our faith or develop our character. Satan tempts us to make us fall. God does not traffic in the realm of the immoral. James points out that God is not even indirectly involved in our sin or temptations, and he states two reasons why: one, *God cannot be tempted by evil.* God in his very nature is holy, there is nothing in him for sin to appeal to; and second, He therefore, does not tempt anyone else. Temptation and our response to it are strictly a matter of personal responsibility.

God has created us as free creatures, and as free creatures, the possibility always exists for us to do wrong. As free creatures, we always have a choice to go to the right or to the left, to choose good or to choose evil. God does not compel us to well doing, or we would cease to be free. Second Corinthians 5:14 tells us, *"For the love of Christ compels us."*

Does the employer tempt the trusted employee to wrongdoing by placing him in charge of his financial affairs? No, but it is a position that has the potential, if the employee so chooses. In like manner, God places us in a position of trust. Trust of necessity involves the possibility of betrayal; it involves the potential for us to do wrong; but may we therefore say that God tempts us to do wrong? No. The choice is ours whether we will, or whether we will not succumb to temptation.

Evil has no place in God. There is nothing in Him that temptation can take hold. Therefore, He will not and cannot solicit us towards what is opposed to His own nature. He tries and tests us; but He does not tempt us. He does not cause sin; he simply permits it. When we pray, as Christ has taught us to do, *"Lead us not into temptation,"* we beg that God in His providence may not place us in circumstances where our hearts may take occasion to sin.

Do not blame God for temptation, He is too holy to be tempted, and His love too great to tempt others. God is not tempted with evil, and he does not tempt to evil. Therefore, we must attribute it not to the Father of lights, but to the prince of darkness. It is the devil, Satan, the deceiver who draws us to take "the easy way out," who draws us to take the path of least resistance. Satan entices us to achieve the good by dishonest means.

TEMPTATION FOLLOWS A CONSISTENT PATTERN.

> *"But each one is tempted when he is drawn away by his own desires and enticed. Then, when desire has conceived, it gives birth to sin; and sin, when it is full-grown, brings forth death."* (vs. 14, 15)

We think of sin as a single act, but God sees it as a process. James described this process, this genesis of sin in four stages:

The first stage is desire—our appetite draws us toward evil indulgence.

God has given us the normal desires of life, and of themselves, they are not sinful. Without these desires, we could not function.

- Unless we felt hunger and thirst, we would never eat and drink, and we would die
- Without fatigue, the body would never rest and would eventually wear out
- Sex is a normal desire; without it, the human race could not continue

It is when we want to satisfy these desires in ways outside God's will that we get into trouble. The Bible says,

- Eating is normal; gluttony is sin
- Sleep is normal; laziness is sin
- Sex in marriage is honorable (Hebrews 13:4); sex apart from marriage is sin

The secret is constant control. These desires must be our servants and not our masters; this we can do only through Jesus Christ.

The second stage deals with our will. Our will yields to the desire, which thus becomes pregnant with action.

Temptation always carries with it some bait that appeals to our natural desires (James must have been fishing when this came to him). Desire is like a hook with its bait that first entices its prey and then drags it away. The bait not only attracts us, but it also hides the fact that yielding to the desire will eventually bring sorrow and punishment. The bait is the exciting thing. The bait keeps us from seeing the consequences of sin. The devil knows the precise bait each of us prefers. He knows exactly where your weakness is. He has been fishing for souls longer than anyone else has on earth. He knows our weaknesses in appetite, and spends time trying to get us to strike at his bait. When we shop advertisers know exactly what attracts us.

Christian living is a matter of the will, not the feelings. Children operate on their feelings, but mature adults operate according to their will. Mature adults act because it is right, no matter how they feel. The more we exercise your will in saying a decisive "No" to temptation, the more we allow God to take control of our lives.

So often, we say "Maybe" to sin instead of "No." We leave the option open for us to say, "Yes." This is not resisting Satan.

We are like the person trying to get rid of a salesperson at the door of their house who does not say a firm "No" and close the door. We say we are not interested in buying the product, but we leave the door ajar, continuing to discuss the product with the salesperson. We are leaving open the possibility for him to make a sale until we say a firm "No" and shut the door.

In the third stage is sin is born, the offspring of the unhallowed union between will and desire or lust.

Desire conceives a method for taking the bait. Desire may be said to "*conceive*," when it obtains the consent of the will. The will approves and acts; and the result is sin. Whether we feel it or not, we are hooked and trapped, and sin is born. Those who dally with temptation, instead of meeting it with instant and prayerful resistance, will eventually succumb to it. From the union of desire with the will, a living sin is born. Jesus told Peter on the Mount of Transfiguration, *"Watch and pray, lest you enter into temptation. The spirit indeed is willing, but the flesh is weak"* (Mark 14:38).

In this, last stage sin *"when it is full grown, brings forth death."*

Disobedience gives birth to death, not life. It may take years for the sin to mature, but when it does, the result is death. Galatians 6:7 clearly states, *"Do not be deceived, God is not mocked; for whatever a man sows, that he will also reap."* There is ultimately a consequence for all that we do. In some cases, sin might lead to physical death, but James here has in mind spiritual death. Death is the fruit of all sin. Sin kills: peace, hope, usefulness, the conscience, and it kills the soul. As Paul observes in Romans 6:23, *"The wages of sin is death"* Only by God's gracious forgiveness can that result be avoided.

Temptation originates within the heart of the sinner. It is in vain for us to blame our Maker. Sin is not to be excused on the plea of an unfavorable environment--upbringing. You cannot blame it on your neighbor. We sin only when we are "*enticed*" by the bait, and "*drawn away*" by the hook of "*our own desire.*" The world and the devil can only tempt us effectively when they stir up the pool of personal desire and get us to respond.

TEMPTATION FLOURISHES ON INCONSISTENT THINKING.

> *"Do not be deceived, my beloved brethren. Every good gift and every perfect gift is from above, and comes down from the Father of lights, with whom there is no variation or shadow of turning."* (vs. 16, 17)

Believing a lie is often much easier than believing the truth. One of the devil's tricks is to convince us that our Father is holding out on us, that He does not really love us and care for us. Once we start to doubt God's goodness, we will be attracted to Satan's offers; and the natural desires within will reach out for his bait.

Although temptation is inevitable, there are ways we can gain victory over it. Here are three of them.

(1) Victory over temptation comes through dwelling on the good.

Our father has provided us from above with "good things" and "perfect gifts." Therefore, to reap good we must dwell on the good. We must get our minds under control and think on things that promote our spiritual well-being. Some dwell on the negative things in life. Paul in Philippians 4:8 would say it this way, *"Finally, brethren, whatever things are true, whatever things are noble, whatever things are just, whatever things are pure, whatever things are lovely, whatever things are of good report, if there is any virtue and if there is anything praiseworthy—meditate on these things."*

God's gifts are always better than Satan's bargains. Satan never gives any gifts, because you end up paying for them dearly.

(2) Victory over temptation comes through living the truth.

The Bible is the only book on earth that presents reliable counsel for exercising consistent victory over temptation. If we put the truth into our minds, then we will counteract evil thoughts. God's word is truth because it does not change. God does not change. The theological word is "immutable."

- He cannot change for the worse because He is holy
- He cannot change for the better because He is already perfect

The light of the sun varies as the earth rotates, but the sun itself is still shining. If shadows come between the Father and us, he did not cause them.

(3) Victory over temptation comes through being born again.

In the closing verse of this passage, verse 18, James says, *"Of His own will He brought us forth by the word of truth, that we might be a kind of firstfruits of His creatures."* Firstfruits is a customary New Testament designation of Christians.

The solution for temptation is to be found in a close relationship with the Father because of new birth. Just as we did not generate our human birth, we cannot generate our spiritual birth. When we put our faith in Jesus Christ, God performs the miracle of our new birth.

- It is a gracious work of God in us
- We cannot earn it and we do not deserve it; God gives us spiritual birth because of His own grace and will
- No one can be born again because of his relatives, his resolutions, or his religion
- The new birth is the work of God
- It is through God's Word

Just as human birth requires two parents, so divine birth has two parents: the Word of God and the Spirit of God. The Spirit of God uses the Word of God to bring about the miracle of the new birth. The new birth that helps us overcome temptation. If we let the old nature, our physical nature (from the first birth) take over, we will fail. We received our old nature (the flesh) from Adam, and he was a failure. However, if we yield to the new nature, our spiritual nature, we will succeed; for that new nature comes from Christ, and He is the Victor.

****

Someone has said, and I do not know if it is true, that the Baltimore Orioles of 1894-96 was the best team baseball had seen to that time, and the craftiest. One of Baltimore's favorite tricks was to plant a few baseballs in strategic spots in the tall outfield grass. Any balls hit in that area that looked as if they would go for extra bases were miraculously held to singles.

One day, however, an opposing batter drove a ball to left of center field where one of the balls had been hidden. The left fielder picked up the hidden ball and threw it in. The center fielder, not seeing what his teammate did picked up the hit ball and threw it in. The umpire, seeing two balls coming into second base, called time and then awarded the game to the visiting team by forfeit.

The Baltimore Orioles tried to take "the easy way out" and it cost them the game. In the game of life, we are called to play by the rules. God has set them down in His playbook of life called the Bible. Any attempt to get around them, to cheat, not only causes us to lose the game, but will stunt our spiritual growth. If we try to take "the easy way out" it may cost us our lives. It may cost us our freedom, our family, but surely, it will cost us our relationship with our heavenly father.

Of all the creatures God has in this universe, Christians are the highest and the finest! We share God's nature. For this reason, it is beneath our dignity to accept Satan's bait or to desire sinful things.

Temptations may be regarded:

- As a test from God to prove us
- As a discipline from God to improve us
- As a temptation from Satan to entice us

Temptation can have no power, unless it meets with some response in us. Thus, we have no right to charge our sins upon God, or make God the author of temptations. The outward occasion may indeed be from him, sent both as a test or a discipline; but the inward inclination, that which leads us away and entices us, is entirely evil and from Satan. No matter what excuses we make, we have no one to blame for sin but ourselves. Our own desires lead us into temptation and sin. God is not to blame.

REFLECTIONS AND MEDITATIONS

1. In what areas of life have you been tempted to take the easy way out?
2. Do you recognize that there are specific areas where you are susceptible to sin?
3. When faced with temptation, in what ways do your thoughts change to combat temptation?

CHAPTER 4

"DO WANT TO BE BLESSED?"

James 1:22-25

> Those who do not take an inventory of their life may find themselves spiritually bankrupt.
>
> *But he who looks into the perfect law of liberty and continues in it, and is not a forgetful hearer but a doer of the work, this one will be blessed in what he does. (James 1:25)*

There is a proverb in the business world that says, "The person who takes no inventories finally becomes bankrupt." If you never take inventory of your life, you may eventually find yourself physically, emotionally, and spiritually bankrupt. Each time we hear the Word of God, we need to take a spiritual inventory. Each of us needs to ask ourselves, "Is he talking to me?"

In this passage, James is not writing to non-Christians or unbelievers. He is writing to good church members, to those who profess Christ as Lord and Savior, who have possibly deceived themselves into believing that regular church attendance is all that is required in the Christian life. It is a plea for vital Christianity. It is a plea for those who claim to know God to take an inventory, to take a good look at themselves. James tells us the Holy Scripture, the Word of God, is a mirror, in which each of us may see our own image reflected. If the Word of God is truly in us there ought to be some sign, some evidence, and some outward demonstration.

Do you want to be blessed? Meaning do you want

- To enjoy the happiness of heaven here on earth
- To be led of God to prosper in all that you do
- To invoke God's favor on your life (and favor is better than money)
- To be guarded and protected of God

Then we must not only hear the Word by apply it to everyday life situations. We must not only hear what is said, but each of us must take a spiritual inventory. We must examine our lives in light of what we hear. In each sermon that we hear each of us needs to ask, "Is he talking to me?" We need to take a spiritual inventory.

Let us follow along with James as he leads us through an example of the man in the mirror that we might take inventory of our lives lest we find ourselves bankrupt of God's blessings.

THE PURPOSE OF PREACHING.

> *But be doers of the word, and not hearers only, deceiving yourselves.* (vs. 22)

Everyone in the community knew George and loved him. Because of his wholehearted commitment to Christ and His church, George's life was a model of integrity and humble Christian service. Whenever there was a need in the community, George was there to do whatever he could. He was not an educated man, but in his own way, he had gained great wisdom that allowed him to translate the teachings of the Bible into practical Christian living. However, George had a problem. He was a farmer who spent most of his waking hours doing hard manual labor outdoors. As a result, when he came to church he had trouble staying awake. Almost every Sunday he was sound asleep before the preacher was five minutes into his sermon. Moreover, to make matters worse, his sleep often was punctuated by deep, resonant snores. Finally, one of the more godly women in the church went to the minister and complained. "It's a disgrace," she said. "He never hears a word of your sermons." "I suppose you are right," chuckled the minister. "But I don't worry. By the life he lives, it appears to me that he hears more of my sermons while he is asleep than most of the rest of the congregation when they are awake."

Many people have the idea that hearing a good sermon or being exposed to Bible study is what makes them grow and receive God's blessings. Yes, they are essential for growth, but it is not the hearing but the doing that brings the blessing. Too many Christians mark their Bibles: red, blue, green with notes and references, but their bibles never mark them. We get in the Word, but the Word never gets in us. If we think we are spiritual because we hear the Word, then we are only kidding ourselves. Those who only hear are self-deceivers. It is not enough to hear the Word we must do it.

The purpose of preaching is not for that the hearer be "very much pleased," but that we may be profited, edified, and inspired to live an upright, generous, and godly life. The Word is not always meant to be a word of comfort and consolation. For the Word will not only comfort the afflicted, but also afflict the comfortable. Some of us ought to leave church sometimes upset with the preacher for having stepped on our toes. For having gotten in our business, for having got right in the middle of that argument with our spouse.

Every preacher wants to feel that he is feeding the flock. However, the highest praise that can be bestowed is not to just tell him how much his preaching is enjoyed on Sunday, but to let him see how well it is being translated into our lives on the other days of the week. Like the man who said, "Pastor that was a good sermon you preached about faithfulness to my wife." However, on Sunday evening he is out with his girlfriend.

Our first responsibility as Christians is to receive the Word. Then, we must practice the Word. Otherwise, we are deceiving ourselves and our claim to be followers of Christ is an empty claim.

WHAT IS THE PROPER USE OF THE WORD OF GOD?

> *For if anyone is a hearer of the word and not a doer, he is like a man observing his natural face in a mirror;* (vs. 23)

The proper use we are to make of God's Word may be learned from its being compared to a mirror in which a person may behold their natural face. There are three ministries of the Word of God as a mirror.

The first ministry of the Word is examination. The main purpose for owning a mirror is to be able to see yourself and make yourself look as clean and neat as possible. As we look into the mirror of God's Word, we see ourselves as we really are. As a mirror shows us the spots and pollutions upon our faces, that they may be remedied and washed off, so the Word of God shows us our sins that we may repent of them. It shows us what is wrong, that it may be changed. Examination is but the first ministry of the mirror of the Word.

There is a second ministry: restoration. The mirror of the Word not only examines us and reveals our sins, but it helps to cleanse us as well. It gives us the promise of cleansing. First John 1:9 declares, *"If we confess our sins, He is faithful and just to forgive us our sins and to cleanse us from all unrighteousness."* As we meditate on it, it cleanses the heart and the mind from spiritual pollution. The blood of Jesus cleanses the guilt, but the water of the Word helps us to wash away the pollution and restores us.

If we stop with examination and restoration, we miss the full benefit of the mirror ministry of the Word. The third ministry is transformation. After Jesus cleanses and restores us, He wants to change us so that we will grow in grace and not commit that sin again. When a believer spends time looking into the Word of God they see the Son of God, and are transformed by the Spirit of God to share in the glory of God!" Too many Christians confess their sins, and claim forgiveness, but never grow spiritually to conquer self and sin. What God wants is for us to be transformed.

If we are to be transformed, we must understand there is a difference between confession and repentance. We can confess, we can say we are sorry for anything, but true repentance is turning away from that sin and living in obedience to God. God is not stupid. He knows if we are truly sorry or just saying words.

- Too many are confessing faithfulness and still committing adultery.
- Too many are confessing abstinence and still engaged in fornication.
- Too many are confessing and are repeatedly doing the same things.

We need to be transformed. Some people are only going through the motions on their way to Hell.

As we meditate on the Word, the Spirit renews the mind and reveals the glory of God. We do not become spiritual overnight. It is a process. The Spirit of God works through the mirror of the Word of God.

WHO THEY ARE THAT DO NOT USE IT AS THEY OUGHT.

> *"For he observes himself, goes away, and immediately forgets what kind of man he was."* (vs. 24)

This is a true description of one who hears the Word of God and does it not. Some people when they sit under the Word are affected with their own sinfulness, misery, and danger. They acknowledge the evil of sin, and their need of Christ; but, when their hearing is over, all is forgotten, convictions are lost, good affections vanish and pass away like the waters of a land-flood. In the words of James, they *"immediately forget."*

James mentions several mistakes people make as they look into God's mirror:

- *They merely glance at themselves.* Many people do not study themselves as they read the Word. They see the faults of others, but not themselves.
- *They forget what they see.* If they were looking deeply enough into their hearts what they would see would be unforgettable.
- *They fail to obey what the Word tells them to do.* They think that hearing is the same as doing, and it is not. We Christians enjoy substituting reading for doing, or even talking for doing, but doing is doing and there is no substitute.

If we are to use God's mirror profitably, we must take the time to examine our hearts and lives in the light of God's Word. This requires time, attention, and sincere devotion. When Jesus examines us. He uses his Word; and he wants us to give him sufficient time to do the job well.

Perhaps one reason we glance into the Word instead of gaze into the Word is that we are afraid of what we might see. Some people will not go to the doctor for an examination for fear of what he might say. Some people will not look under the hood of their car for fear of what they might find wrong. Some people will not inquire into the activities of their children for fear they might be doing something that they really would rather not know about. Some of us are afraid to inquire truly into the things of God, to read and study the Bible, for fear of what we might see, for fear of what we might find, or for fear of what changes we may have to make.

However, if we would be blessed we must look intently and intensely. Moreover, after seeing ourselves, we must remember who and whose we are, what we are, what God says we must do according to the Word. The blessing comes in the doing, not in just the reading of the Word.

WHO ARE THEY THAT MAKE RIGHT USE OF IT?

> *But he who looks into the perfect law of liberty and continues in it, and is not a forgetful hearer but a doer of the work, this one will be blessed in what he does.* (vs. 25)

Why does James call the Word of God "the perfect law of liberty?" Because when we obey it, God sets us free. John 8:34 declares, "*Whoever commits sin is a slave of sin.*" Jesus said in John 8:31-32, *"If you abide in My word, you are My disciples indeed." And you shall know the truth, and the truth shall make you free."*

The Word of God is perfect in the sense that it is free of defects, and it is a law of liberty because it is capable of freeing people from the pain and passions of sin. However, a person must not only look at the Word of God but must remember to obey it.

At any school, college, or university, you have an option to enroll for credit or to audit a class. The one who audits listens and takes note, but has no assignments, no responsibilities, and no tests. Some of us I fear have signed up for "church" to audit the worship service. We do not intend to do any significant work, of putting forth any real effort to change, of researching or looking for truth beyond what we hear in the assembly. Some of us I fear are only desire "to hear" what is said, digest it if we think it tastes good and does not convict us too much, and spit it out or forget it if it does. James declares this person is not in a position to be blessed.

Some folks are caught up just in the hearing. They hear this person today, tomorrow another, and they get so busy and wrapped up in hearing that they fail to digest and apply what they have heard. They never get to the point, having heard other folks, of arriving at their own conclusions. What they have heard has no influence on their lives. They are just as ornery and hard to get along with as they have always been, still engaged in lustful activities, and still wrapped up in their own thing. Instead of bringing harmony to a situation, they breed discord and strife. They are swift to hear; they are also swift to condemn, swift to get angry. There is an inconsistency here, and that inconsistency is the difference between hearing and doing.

What does your spiritual inventory say today? Are you a just a hearer, or are you also a doer? Those who continue in obedience to the law of God, who are not forgetful of it, but practice it as our work and business, and make it the constant rule of our conversation and behavior, are, and shall be, blessed in our deeds; blessed in all our ways.

****

The druggist of the town overheard a young boy talking on a pay telephone. "Hello, sir, I was calling to see if you needed a lawn boy. Oh, you have one. Well, is he any good? Oh, he is! Thank you, I was just checking," said the young boy. The druggist then said to the boy, "Sorry you didn't get the job, son." "Oh, no sir," said the boy, "I've got the job. I was just checking up on myself."

Some of us need to check up on ourselves. Some of us need to inquire honestly, as to what other saints of God think about us. We need to take a spiritual inventory. We need to take some time and sit back and think about our attitudes and our actions. Think about where we are really going with this thing of Christianity. Honestly evaluate what we are about, where we are going, and how we plan to get there in light of the required obedience of God's Word.

Paul says in 1 Corinthians 1:18, *"For the message of the cross is foolishness to those who are perishing, but to us who are being saved it is the power of God."* It pleased God by the foolishness of preaching to save them that believe.

Some of you have been going from church to church, hearing this preacher and that preacher. Some of you have thought good, others not so good. Nevertheless, what change has it made in your life? Have you only heard about the salvation in Jesus Christ, have you only heard about God's love for you, have you only heard that you need to let go and let God come into your life? I challenge you to stop being a hearer only and become a doer today.

REFLECTIONS AND MEDITATIONS

1. What purpose has preaching made towards change in your life?
2. What has the mirror of the Word of God revealed that needs to change in your life?
3. Does conviction by the Word of God bring lasting desire to change, or is it just a temporary inconvenience?
4. Is there inconsistency between your hearing and doing?

CHAPTER 5

"SPIRITUAL INCOMPATIBILITY"

James 2:1-9

> Within the sacred circle of our church life, respect is to be paid to religious character and not to material wealth.

> *My brethren, do not hold the faith of our Lord Jesus Christ, the Lord of glory, with partiality. (James 2:1)*

One day, a financially comfortable father decided to take his son to the country with the purpose of showing him how poor people live. His purpose was that the son could understand the value of things and realize how fortunate they were.

They stayed overnight at a very humble family's farm for one day and one night. As the trip ended, and during their return home, the father asks his son, "So what did you think of the trip?" "It was great, dad!" "Did you see how poor and needy some people have to live?" "Yes!" "And what did you learn?"

> "I saw that we have one dog in the house, but they have four
> We have a huge swimming pool, but they have a river that never ever ends

> We have imported lamps in the patio, they have the stars
> Our backyard ends at the fence, but theirs goes on and on into the horizon

Especially though, dad, I saw that they have time to talk to each other and live as a family. You and Mom have to work all day, and I hardly see you both!" As the conversation ended, the father remained silent, and his son added, "Thanks Dad, for showing me how rich we could be!"[5]

In this passage, James admonishes us that we cannot claim that we belong to the Lord Jesus Christ, the Lord of glory, if we show favoritism to rich people and look down on poor people. We cannot say we have faith in Christ and show partiality. Faith and partiality are incompatible. If faith and partiality are incompatible that means they are incapable of coexisting harmoniously. They disagree in nature. They are in conflict.

The term partiality, or favoritism used by James comes from two Greek words combined to mean, "to receive by face" and has the thought of accepting or welcoming someone by face value alone. He is talking about favoritism shown another person based on an initial encounter.

James urges that within the sacred circle of our church life respect is to be paid to religious character and not to material wealth. To help us understand how this partiality might be seen in the church, James in verses 2 through 4 gives us an illustration. *"For if there should come into your assembly a man with gold rings, in fine apparel, and there should also come in a poor man in filthy clothes, and you pay attention to the one wearing the fine clothes and say to him, "You sit here in a good place," and say to the poor man, "You stand there," or, "Sit here at my footstool," have you not shown partiality among yourselves, and become judges with evil thoughts?"* (vs. 2-4)

---

5 http://www.sermoncentral.com/illustrations/sermon-illustration-steve-miller-stories-poverty-perspective-19640.asp

The assembly to which James refers is the meeting of Christians. Possibly, it was a scene where the believers had met for worship, and the usher at the door noticed two different people looking for seats: one a wealthy man, the other poor. Presumably, both the rich man and the poor man who came to the meeting were strangers. The rich man wore a gold ring, a symbol of wealth in the Orient, and goodly apparel, fine clothes that would be especially conspicuous in a church gathering where most people were quite poor. The poor man was equally conspicuous by what he wore.

The usher was faced with a choice; where does he seat these two people. Matthew 23:6 helps us better to understand this situation by telling us that there were chief seats in the synagogues. The Pharisees loved the chief seats apparently located down in front because they could enter the place of worship in their elegant robes and march toward the front, calling attention to themselves. Jewish people in that day coveted recognition and honor, and competed with another for praise. We would not be guilty of that would we?

Faced with the decision of seating one or the other in the available seat the usher yielded to a judgment based upon externals only. The rich man was immediately ushered to the best seat. Great honor was paid without any reference to his character, simply because he appeared to be rich. The poor man was given the choice to sit on the floor or to stand off to the side.

James describes the motives for such a decision as *"evil."* By showing partiality based on outward appearance, these Christians were behaving in a manner that was clearly wicked. It is wrong to show favoritism to a person because of his or her social status, race, or language. God shows no favoritism (Romans 2:11; Ephesians 6:9, Colossians 3:25); therefore, neither should Christians. God does not respect faces. Whereas people judge by the face, God judges by the heart. [6]

---

6 John F. Walvoord and Roy B. Zuck, ed, *The Bible Knowledge Commentary*, New Testament Edition (Colorado Springs, CO: Victor Books, 1983), 824

We must be careful not to apply what is here said of the common assemblies for worship; for in these certainly there may be appointed different places of persons according to their rank and circumstances, without sin. However, in matters of religion, rich and poor stand upon level ground. Riches did not set a person in the least nearer to God, nor does any persons poverty set them at a distance from God. With the Most High, there is no respect of persons, and therefore in matters of conscience there should be none with us.

James gives us three good reasons for not being involved in practicing partiality.

THEOLOGICAL REASON: GOD IS NO RESPECTER OF PERSONS.

James asks the question, *"Has God not chosen the poor of this world to be rich in faith and heirs of the kingdom which He promised to those who love Him*" (vs. 5)? A careful look at James thoughts reveals that from God's perspective the real issue is not wealth or poverty, but the condition of one's soul. God looks at the heart. We ought to ask ourselves, "If God were welcoming men and women on face value alone, would he have accepted me and asked me to be part of his family?"

When Jesus lived on earth, was no flatterer of the rich. He was himself a poor man. He did not respect persons. Even his enemies admitted, *"Teacher, we know that You are true, and teach the way of God in truth; nor do You care about anyone, for You do not regard the person of men"* (Matt 22:16). Our Lord did not look at the outward appearances; he looked at the heart. He was not impressed with riches or social status. He saw the potential in the lives of sinners.

- The poor widow who gave her mite was greater in his eyes than the rich Pharisee who boastfully gave his large donation
- In Simon a lowly fisherman, he saw a rock. One who played a significant part in the foundation of the church

- In Matthew, the Publican-a despised tax collector, he saw a faithful disciple who would one day write one of the four gospels
- The disciples were amazed to see Jesus talking to a despised Samaritan woman at the well of Sychar, but Jesus saw in her an instrument for reaping a great harvest.

The religious experts in Christ's day judged him by their human standards, and they rejected him.

- Unlike the foxes and the birds, he had no home
- He came from the wrong city, Nazareth of Galilee, from a home that knew the meaning of poverty
- He was not a graduate of the accepted schools
- He did not have the approval of the people in power
- He had no wealth
- His followers were an indistinct mob and included publicans and sinners

Sad to say, we often make the same mistakes. Had you and I met him while he was ministering on earth, we would have seen nothing physically and materially that would attract us. Yet, he was the very glory of God!

We are also prone to judge by the outward appearance than by the inner attitudes of the heart. Many times dress, color of skin, fashion, and other superficial things carry more weight than the fruit of the spirit that may be manifested in their lives. We cater to the rich because we sometimes hope to get something from them. We desire to be the beautiful people that we see portrayed on television, and we avoid the poor because they embarrass us. Jesus did not do this and he cannot approve of it.

If there is a privileged group in the church, it is the very poor whom the church was treating shamefully. God often has selected the poor to be the recipients of his special favors. The size of a person's bank account is not an accurate measure of their faith.

We should look at everyone through the eye of Christ. If the visitor is a Christian, we can accept him because Christ lives in him. If he is not a Christian, we can receive him because Christ died for him.

Abraham Lincoln said that God must love common people because he made so many of them. The Lord loves poor people, too. God's message for the poor is that if they will set their love on him, they may become heirs of his Kingdom. He will make them "rich in faith." This true wealth cannot fade away and is reserved in heaven for those to whom it belongs. It is available to the rich on exactly the same terms as to the poor. God loves the poor and accepts them as readily as he accepts the rich, but some Christians were dishonoring the poor and favoring the rich.

A LOGICAL REASON: THE RICH AS A CLASS HAD BEEN THE ENEMIES OF BOTH CHRIST AND HIS PEOPLE.

> *"But you have dishonored the poor man. Do not the rich oppress you and drag you into the courts? Do they not blaspheme that noble name by which you are called?"* (vs. 6, 7)

The poor could not afford a lawyer; and besides, the rich often bought off the judges. In those days, persons could be thrown into jail or even sold into slavery for failing to pay their debts.

The people in James's audience were strangely exalting the very ones who were bringing them pain and injury. These people were dangerous because they were driven by blatant unbelief. James argues that the church dishonors the poor man by showing partiality to the rich man who so often oppresses not only the poor but also those who bow and scrape before him when he comes to church. Of course, James is not saying that all the rich people are oppressors. In fact, some are most gracious and generous. Yet it is a readily observed fact that the rich, not the poor, are most often the oppressors.

James lodges one final charge against the rich persecutors. They blaspheme the very name of Christ that the Christians proudly bear. It may seem hard to believe that Christians would give honor to those who dishonor the Lord. Yet the worldly prestige that is enjoyed by being associated with the rich will cause some persons to overlook such blasphemy and cater to the blasphemers.

BIBLICAL REASON: IT IS INCONSISTENT WITH SCRIPTURE.

> *"If you really fulfill the royal law according to the Scripture, "You shall love your neighbor as yourself," you do well; but if you show partiality, you commit sin, and are convicted by the law as transgressors"* (vs. 8, 9)

Lest any should think James had been pleading for the poor to have contempt on the rich, he now lets them know that he did not intend to encourage improper conduct towards them. They must not hate nor be rude to the rich, any more than despise the poor; but as the scripture teaches us to love all our neighbors, be they rich or poor, as ourselves.

One well-known law was given by Moses and said, *"You shall love you neighbor as yourself"* (Leviticus 19:18). The exercise of partiality was an outright contradiction of that law. Such a contradiction between the biblical standard and our behavior James called sin—the transgressing of the law. If we arrange James' words into a personal message to ourselves, we can say, "If I show partiality or prejudice because of face (surface) relationships, I sin!"

The important question is not, "Who is my neighbor?" However, to whom can I be a neighbor? "Love thy neighbor" is the royal law for a second reason; it rules all other laws. "Love is the fulfilling of the law" (Romans 13:10). There would be no need for the thousands of complex laws if each citizen truly loved his neighbor.

Christian love does not mean that I must like a person and agree with them on everything. I may not like their vocabulary or their habits, and I may not want them for an intimate friend. Christian love means treating others as God has treated me. It is an act of the will, not an emotion, which I try to manufacture. The motive is to glorify God.

Christian love does not leave the person where it finds them. Love should help the poor person do better. Love should help the rich person make better use of his God-given resources. Love always builds up (1 Corinthians 8:1); hatred always tears down.

Are not all of us, in one way or another, guilty of this transgression? We may show favoritism to some and not to others openly, even blatantly. Sometimes our favoritism may be subtle, or even unconscious. We need constantly to work at sensitizing ourselves so that we are not guilty of this transgression. No matter how we regard it, God considers it sin.

****

A tax assessor came one day to a poor Christian to determine the amount of taxes he would have to pay. The following conversation took place: "What property do you possess?" asked the assessor. "I am a very wealthy man," replied the Christian. "List your possessions, please," the assessor instructed. The Christian said:

- First, I have everlasting life, John 3:16
- Second, I have a mansion in heaven, John 14:2
- Third, I have peace that passes all understanding, Philippians 4:7
- Fourth, I have joy unspeakable, 1 Peter 1:8
- Fifth, I have divine love which never fails, 1 Corinthians 13:8
- Sixth, I have a faithful wife, Proverbs 31:10
- Seventh, I have healthy, happy obedient children, Exodus 20:12
- Eighth, I have true, loyal friends, Proverbs 18:24
- Ninth, I have songs in the night, Psalms 42:8
- Tenth, I have a crown of life, James 1:12

The tax assessor closed his book, and said, "Truly you are a very rich man, but your property is not subject to taxation."

James teaches us that the grace of God makes the rich man poor, because he cannot depend on his wealth; and it makes the poor man rich, because he inherits the riches of grace in Christ.

It all depends on what we do with Christ and the materials and wealth he has given to us. God promises the kingdom to "those that love him" (James 2:5), not to those who love this world and its riches.

Those who assemble in the house of God are the guests of *"the Lord of Glory."* That means that when we as frail creatures, no matter what our social status, come before an Almighty God, the Lord of glory, we all spiritually stand on level ground. There are no big "I's" or little "you's."

As Christians must always act toward others based on what we are, and not according to what they may or may not be. God accepts us based on what are in Christ Jesus. If salvation were based on merit, it would not be by grace. Grace, the unmerited favor of God, implies God's sovereign choice of those who cannot earn and do not deserve his salvation. God saves us completely regardless of what we are or have.

- God ignores national differences
- God ignores social differences
- Masters, slaves, rich, and poor are alike to him

Wealth and position should not merit special privileges within the church. The people told to sit on the floor may be the very persons God honors. God does not measure persons by the cut of their clothes, the size of their bank account, or the luxury of their dwellings. God's concern is not with what a person has, but with what a person is. A rich person can be just as poor in spirit as an impoverished person can; a poor man can be just as devilish as a rich man can. What one has in his heart is more important than the clothes that cover his chest.

REFLECTIONS AND MEDITATIONS

1. Have your ever been guilty of accepting one person over another based on physical appearance?
2. Are you a better friend to the rich than the poor?
3. Are you extending genuine friendship to others in the same way that you want to receive it?

CHAPTER 6

"WHAT KIND OF FAITH SAVES?"

James 2:14-26

> Out of our faith in Christ must come evidence that God is working and active in our lives.
>
> *"Thus also faith by itself, if it does not have works, is dead." (James 2:17)*

Life is a continuous adventure into the unknown. Faith of some sort, therefore, is necessary. *"By faith"* is the word necessary in each of our lives.

Faith is not some kind of vague feeling that we experience; faith is more than believing in ourselves, or in our abilities. Hebrews 11:1 tells us, *"Now faith is the substance of things hoped for, the evidence of things not seen."* Real faith is confidence that God's Word is true, and conviction that acting upon the Word will bring blessings in our lives.

In this passage, James enlightens us on the relationship between faith and works. This is an important discussion, for if we are wrong in this matter, we jeopardize our eternal salvation. If we are wrong in this matter, we can spend a lot of time, energy, and effort in the spiritual pursuit of salvation only to find that we have missed the mark. We want to consider possibly some confusing questions:

- What kind of faith really saves a person?
- Is it necessary to perform good works to be saved?
- How can a person tell whether he or she is exercising true saving faith?

These may seem to be odd questions to most of us, because in our minds we would say that faith is faith, and that faith in the Lord Jesus Christ is what saves. In that understanding, we are correct. However, in this passage James brings before us a distinction as related to the faith that we all claim to have and our works—the practical demonstration of our faith.

In three verses of this passage before us, James makes it very clear that *faith without works is dead.*

FAITH AND WORKS IN CONFLICT?

> *"What does it profit, my brethren, if someone says he has faith but does not have works? Can faith save him?"* (vs. 14)
>
> *"Thus also faith by itself, if it does not have works, is dead."* (vs. 17)

Many have missed the thrust of James message, thinking it contradicts the apostle Paul's message of justification by faith as addressed in the book of Romans. In Romans 3:28, Paul wrote, *"A man is justified by faith without the deeds of the law."* This is to say the lost person. The person who has not received Christ, as their personal savior is declared righteous, or in right relationship, by God's grace apart from works. It is the gift of God.

In contrast, James announced that a person is justified, presented before God just-as-if they had never sinned or sinless, by works in conjunction with faith and not by faith alone. At this point James may seem to be in disagreement with Paul. Consider, though, the kinds of "works" of which they were talking.

Certain people who insisted that the rituals of the Old Testament law: circumcision, the keeping of feast and fasts, and the offering of sacrifices were necessary to salvation, even in Christ, confronted Paul. Paul responded that salvation in Christ required none of these things.

James, on the other hand, faced the problem of people who "believed" in Jesus Christ but still acted, especially toward the needy among them, as though there was no need to exercise their faith in a practical way in meeting the needs of others.

Simply put, Paul met with many people who made works everything, to the neglect of faith; and James met with others who made faith everything, to the neglect of works.

James said that there are things that should happen in the life of a believer, indicating that they are indeed saved. That is to say,

- If you are saved
- If you have been adopted into the royal family of God
- If Christ is on the throne of your heart there ought to be some sign

James is saying that a person's works validate them as a genuine believer.

James implies plainly that we are not saved by the kind of faith that does not produce good works, but he makes it clear that salvation is by faith, or by believing. Yes, faith, not good works, is responsible for salvation-but God wants good works to follow our being saved. Ephesians 2:10 tells us that, *"We are his workmanship, created in Christ Jesus unto good works, which God hath before ordained that we should walk in them."*

The very faith that saves us is a faith that brings forth after-fruits, or it is not true faith at all. So then, the "works" to which Paul refers are works done with a view of salvation, that somehow God's favor may be won by them. The works to which James refers are works springing out of salvation, because God's favor has been so freely and graciously bestowed.

FAITH AND WORKS MUST WORK HAND IN HAND.

> *"But do you want to know, O foolish man, that faith without works is dead?"* (vs. 20)

An old story is told that tells about two preachers who were being rowed across a river. They discussed the relative importance of faith and works. When the boatman saw that the "two reverends" could not reconcile their views, he undertook to settle the dispute but did not quite get it right. He said, "It's like this, gentlemen. The oar in my right hand is faith; the oar in my left hand is works. If I pull only on the oar of faith, you see the boat goes around in circles. If I use only the oar of works in my left hand, we go in circles in the opposite direction. However, when I pull on both oars, you see we go straight toward our destination. So, gentlemen, it is not faith without works, not works without faith, but, as James said, faith with works." [7]

His explanation needs to be clarified in this manner. James does not say works without faith saves us, but neither does he tell us we are saved by faith plus works. What he says is that the kind of faith that saves is the kind that produces good works. God saves us so that we may live a life of good works (Ephesians 2:10). He equips us, by giving us His Holy Spirit, for this sort of life (Philippians 2:14). If we fail to produce good works that are to accompany faith, we are to examine ourselves carefully (2 Corinthians 13:5) to make sure that we have genuine faith rather than the kind that James condemns as "useless" and "dead." However, it is always the faith, not the works that saves us. Works are important as evidence of faith, but they have no saving value whatever.

---

[7] Walter B. Knight, *Knight's Master Book of New Illustrations* (Grand Rapids, MI: William B. Eerdmans Publishing Co., 1986) 195.

Like the paired wings of a bird, like the mated oars of a boat, like the left hand to the right—such is the relationship of faith and works. Neither is complete without the other. The bird may as well attempt to fly with a single wing, or the oarsmen to row a straight course with a single oar, or the laborer to perform complicated work efficiently with a single hand, as to expect genuine faith in God to appear in a life that is void of works.

Now lest it be misunderstood regarding this thing of works, a word of caution should be inserted here. There is a place for quiet mediation and prayer in the Christian life. Good works without these can degenerate into busy activity that is no more an expression of Christian faith than is passive activity. Someone has revised the old nursery rhyme to read:

> Mary had a little lamb,
> 'Twas given her to keep;
> But then it joined a Baptist Church,
> And died for lack of sleep.

We are not to judge our faith on the number of activities in which we are involved. We should seek balance in all things. The church is like a bank. The more you put into it, the greater the interest you will have in it.

We must also take care lest we come to look upon our own activity as the only true expression of Christian faith while rejecting the activity of others as inadequate. We are not to judge whether other people are saved by whether they can keep up with us or not. We do not want to get into measuring our faith based upon the exercise of our gifts. God has given us different gifts, and it is not our place to pass judgement on how others exercise their gifts. God has given each of us a measure of faith and we need to exercise that faith in the fullest extent in the activity to which he leads us.

HOW CAN I KEEP FAITH ALIVE?

> *"For as the body without the spirit is dead, so faith without works is dead also."* (vs. 26)

After citing two examples of individuals whose faith was validated by their works (Abraham—the father of the Jews, a respected man; and Rahab—a Gentile harlot, a woman "insignificant" to the people), he drove home his point with this succinct statement, *"For as the body without the spirit is dead, so faith without works is dead also"* (vs. 26).

Spiritually,

- When demonstration separates itself from faith
- When there is no outward expression of an inner conversion
- When there is no outward expression that we believe what we say we believe
- When faith has gone into remission in our life

That faith becomes lifeless and useless. That faith becomes a dead faith.

Well, how can I have dynamic faith you may ask? How can we keep faith alive? We must begin to exercise the faith that we claim to have. In order that our faith will become and remain strong and alive

- We must entertain the Word of God daily
- We must develop an ever present awareness, a sense of God's presence and his working in our lives for good
- We must apply the Word to every area of our lives surrendering every area of our lives to God

Why do you go to church? Why have you joined a church? It is hopefully because it had something you needed. Christ is in your life; the warmth and fellowship of other believers; instruction in the things of God. However, I also hope it was because you had something that you wanted to share, something that God had given you that you wanted to give away, a talent, an ability, a service, and our treasure.

The Church is not a grocery store chain. You do not come to buy what you need. It is more of a co-op. We gather to worship and praise God and to encourage one another. You bring what you have. Others come here and bring what they have. And as we share, both of our needs are met. I have heard preachers say, "You bring a lump of coal, and I'll bring a lump of coal, and when we put it all together we set the place on fire."

If you come burdened down and leave the same way, then something is wrong. If you come with problems and do not leave with faith that God can solve them, then something is wrong. Our purpose in coming, apart from worship, should be to encourage one another, to challenge one another to a Christ-like lifestyle, to share one another's burdens. If that is not happening in your life then something is wrong.

- Maybe what you need is to forget your pride, stop carrying the load yourself, and ask God for help
- Maybe what you need is to get off the frontage road and get onto the freeway
- Maybe what you need to do is to get off the fringe of this thing called Christianity and come into the center

Let me illustrate what I am trying to say. A gentleman was invited by a friend into his orchard to test the apples. "No," he said, "I would rather not," and being asked often to come and eat, and yet refusing, the owner said, "I guess you've a prejudice against my apples." "Yes," said the man, "I've tasted a few of them, and they are very sour." "But which," said the owner, "did you taste?" "Why, those apples that fell into the road over the hedge." "Ah, yes," said the owner. "They are as sour as crabs. I planted them for the good of the boys, to keep them out of my orchard, but if you come to the middle of the lot, you will find a different flavor," and so it was.

Now just around the border of religion, along the outer hedge, there are some very sour apples: apples of conviction, self-denial, humiliation, and self-despair, planted on purpose to keep out the hypocrites and mere professors of the faith. However, in the midst of the garden are luscious fruits, mellow to the taste, and sweet as nectar. The central position in religion is sweetest. The nearer to God we become the sweeter the joy.

Some of you do not want to come into the center of what God is all about. You would rather hang around the outside. And out there, you can never taste of God's best. If you want a dynamic faith, if you want to keep faith alive, you must be willing to move beyond being a mere spectator to become an active participant that you can receive what God has for you. *"Draw near to God and He will draw near to you"* (James 4:8).

If you want to have a living and dynamic faith you must come to the center of this Christian thing. You must be willing to give complete and total control of your life to Christ.

****

The story is told of a girl who said she would marry her fellow only "when apples grow on the lilac tree." Early in the morning, the persistent chap was out tying apples on the lilac tree to meet her condition. Good works, however, are not apples to be tied to a lilac tree. The good works God wants will come naturally, not by self-effort, when your relationship to God is what it should be.

What kind of faith do you have? True saving faith involves something more than the intellect. It involves something that can be genuinely seen and recognized as a changed life.

Faith is the key doctrine in the Christian Life. Our whole relationship with God is based upon it.

- We receive the Word and this saves us. *So then faith comes by hearing, and hearing by the word of God* (Romans 10:17)

- The sinner is saved by faith. *"For by grace are ye saved through faith; and that not of yourselves: it is the gift of God: Not of works, lest any man should boast"* (Ephesians 2:8,9)
- The believer must walk by faith. *"For we walk by faith, not by sight"* (2 Corinthians 5:7)
- Without faith, it is impossible to please God. *"But without faith it is impossible to please him: For he that cometh to God must believe that he is, and that he is a rewarder of them that diligently seek him"* (Hebrews 11:6)

If you are saved, if you know that you know, that you know that you know that you have been adopted into the royal family of God, if Christ is on the throne of your heart there ought to be some sign. Our works validate us as genuine believers. Our works take a mere profession of faith and give it life.

Yes, we are without a doubt saved by faith, but we are not saved by the kind of faith that does not produce good works. Yes, faith, not good works, is responsible for our salvation—but God wants our good works to follow our being saved. God wants us to bring what we do into alignment with what we claim to believe. Genuine faith produces genuine works. Good works validate genuine faith. If this is not the case, then the validity of our faith should be questioned.

Talk is cheap. It is easy for anyone to say that he has faith. However, the demonstration of that faith is another matter. Faith without works is like compassion without help. It is devoid of life. Faith without a practical expression in deeds is as empty as "love" without practical expression in acts of mercy. If someone says he or she loves you and never gives you anything, never takes you anywhere, never does anything for you; that is a strange kind of love. That kind of love is one sided, that kind of love lacks unity and harmony. Living faith gets things done. True saving faith leads to action. A faith that does not fill one's heart with love for God, which does not produce any works, is unable to show itself; therefore, it is not faith at all and surely cannot save us.

REFLECTIONS AND MEDITATIONS

1. How are the works of your faith seen?
2. What gifts has God given you that are being used to advance the Kingdom?
3. Are you on the fringe of this thing called Christianity, or have you moved into the center?

CHAPTER 7

"ORAL INCONSISTENCIES"

James 3:1-12

> *"Out of the same mouth proceed blessing and cursing. My brethren, these things ought not to be so." (James 3:10)*

I love you, you are important to me, thank you so much, how can I repay you, you look really nice today, I like your new haircut, great job, this place wouldn't be the same without you, I'm proud of you, you are irreplaceable.

I hate you, you disgust me, I wish you had never been born, I wish I were dead, you make me sick, I want a divorce, nobody cares about you, I will never speak to you again.

The power of speech is one of the greatest powers God has given us. With the tongue, we can praise God, pray, preach the Word, and lead the lost to Christ. What a privilege! However, with that same tongue we can tell lies that could ruin a person's reputation or break a person's heart. It must be constantly monitored lest it burst out of control. It is an unruly evil.

Much has been written much on the subject of the tongue but no other section of the Bible speaks with greater authority or impact regarding this subject than does James.

THE TONGUE, THOUGH SMALL, IS POWERFUL.

The Christians that James wrote to were apparently having serious problems with their tongues. In the development of his thinking, James drew upon three illustrations to know what the tongue is like. James gives some illustrations of small but important objects. Here are James' three illustrations:

A Horse's Bridle.

> *"Indeed, we put bits in horses' mouths that they may obey us, and we turn their whole body."* (vs. 3)

James spoke of an apparatus containing a metal bit which, when placed in the mouth of the horse, it controls every movement of the horse. Without a bit in the horse's mouth it is impossible for the rider to have command and control. The five-pound bit by which we control a horse is rather insignificant in comparison with the bulk of the horse's 1500-pound body, but by it, we cause the animal to go wherever we want him to take us, and stop him when we get there.

In like manner, without a bridle on the tongue, no person can govern himself or herself properly. David felt this, and said, *"I will guard my ways, lest I sin with my tongue; I will restrain my mouth with a muzzle, while the wicked are before me"* (Psalm 39:1).

A Ship's Rudder.

> *"Look also at ships: although they are so large and are driven by fierce winds, they are turned by a very small rudder wherever the pilot desires."* (vs. 4)

A rudder is smaller in proportion to a ship than a bit is to a horse; yet, in spite of its size, it determines the course of the ship as it crosses the powerful ocean currents. By it, the pilot turns the craft and causes it to go in whatever direction he chooses. Both the bit and the rudder must overcome contrary forces. This means that both the bit and the rudder must be under the control of a strong hand. The bit must overcome the wild nature of the horse, and the rudder must fight the winds and currents that would drive the ship off its course.

The human tongue also must overcome contrary forces. We have an old nature that wants to control us and make us sin. There are circumstances that would make us say things we ought not to say. Sin on the inside and pressures on the outside are seeking to get control of the tongue.

A Fire's Spark.

> *"Even so the tongue is a little member and boasts great things. See how great a forest a little fire kindles! And the tongue is a fire, a world of iniquity. The tongue is so set among our members that it defiles the whole body, and sets on fire the course of nature; and it is set on fire by hell."* (vs. 5, 6)

A fire usually has a small beginning. Back in 1871, a cow being milked by a Mrs. O'Leary in a Chicago barn kicked over her lamp and set fire to the hay in the stall, setting off what became the Great Chicago Fire. Before the flames could be controlled, they had destroyed 17,450 buildings, including the entire business district of that great city. More than 250 people were killed.

Although seemingly inconsequential because of its size, the tongue's potential to influence and destroy is far reaching, depending on how it is used. *"Death and life are in the power of the tongue,"* warned Solomon (Proverbs 18:21). No wonder David prayed, *"Set a guard, O Lord, over my mouth; keep watch over the door of my lips. Do not incline my heart to any evil thing"* (Psalm 141:3-4a). David knew that the heart is the key to right speech. *"For out of the abundance of the heart the mouth speaks"* (Matthew 12:34b).

The heart and tongue are directly associated with each other. Through it's every word the tongue telegraphs the condition of the heart. Jesus said in Matthew 15:11, 18-19, *"Not what goes into the mouth defiles a man; but what comes out of the mouth, this defiles a man." "But those things which proceed out of the mouth come from the heart, and they defile a man." "For out of the heart proceed evil thoughts, murders, adulteries, fornications, thefts, false witness, blasphemies."* When Jesus is the Lord of the heart, then He is the Lord of the lips too.

Yes, the tongue is like a bit and a rudder; it has the power to direct. It is like a fire's spark. It is capable of great destruction. How important it is that our tongues direct people in the right way!

THE TONGUE, THOUGH SMALL, IS INFLUENTIAL.

> *"All kinds of animals, birds, reptiles and creatures of the sea are being tamed and have been tamed by man, but no man can tame the tongue. It is a restless evil, full of deadly poison."* (vs. 8, 9)

A man in a small village had been found guilty of starting a malicious rumor about another man. Not only was this rumor untrue, but it seriously damaged the other man's reputation and family. As is often the custom in small villages, the accused was taken before the chief of the village who served as a judge and would hear the case and decide the man's punishment if found guilty.

After hearing the facts of the case, the chief found the accused to be guilty and was now preparing to sentence the man to his punishment. The old, wise chief handed the man a large bag of feathers and told him that his only punishment would be to place a feather on the doorstep of every person to whom he had told the rumor. The man was relieved at such a light punishment and quickly took the bag of feathers and set about his task. Four hours later, the man returned to the king with the empty bag and said, "I completed your task, sir. Is there anything else?"

"Yes, the wise chief replied. Report to me in the morning and I'll give you the second half of your punishment." The man reported the next morning and was instructed that the second half of his punishment was to gather all the feathers back up and place them in the bag. "But sir," the man replied, "didn't you hear the storm that raged through our village last night? Did not you feel the force of the winds that blew? It would be impossible to know where those feathers are now."

The wise old chief raised his index finger and pointed knowingly at the man, "now you see, my child, the damage that you have done to another. For although you told only a few lies here and there, the storm of gossip took hold of those lies and spread them far beyond your grasp to undo them. You can regret what you said, but you can never fully undo what you've said." [8]

It would be hard to tell how many: homes have been saddened, friendships broken, marriages ruined, reputations lost, and futures darkened by the misuse of the tongue. The abuse of the tongue has dashed more hopes and caused more pain than most of us can imagine. No matter how you may regret them or try to "explain" them, you can never "unsay" the words you speak. It would be easier to try to unscramble an egg.

The tongue has vast potentialities for evil. It can poison the whole body; it can make the whole of life a blazing hell. How so you may ask? The sins of speech are many and varied.

There is **LYING**, speaking or acting in such a way as to give an impression that is not true. The story is told of a doctor who was fond of horseback riding named his horse "Consultation." Then, when patients called and wanted to see him at one, his nurse would say, "Sorry—the doctor is out on Consultation."

Then there is **GOSSIP**, or passing on groundless rumors about a person, and slander, or maliciously circulating false reports.

The old nursery rhyme says, "Sticks and stones may break my bones, but names can never hurt me." Is this proverb true? The

---

[8] http://www.sermoncentral.com/*sermons/taming-the-tongue-jeff-simms-sermon-on-character-65944.asp?Page=2 (Story originally told by Greg Warren)*

wounds in the body made by stones may heal, but the hurt in the heart made by an insult may endure for a lifetime.

It is not easy to resist the temptation to gossip, yet as maturing Christians we must learn to do so. We need to think, T.H.I.N.K, before we speak. Before we say what we intend to say we need to ask ourselves the following five questions:

T—Is it true?
H—Is it helpful?
I—Is it inspiring?
N—Is it necessary?
K—Is it kind?

The next time someone comes to you with a juicy bit of gossip, ask him or her these five questions. They are likely to be shocked at first, but once they recover, they will see the fairness of these questions. Is it true? Is it helpful? Is it inspiring? Is it needful? Is it kind?

INDECENT, VULGAR TALK—cheap use of "four-letter words" and **PROFANITY—**taking the Lord's name in vain, are a common sin today—both among the lowest class of people and among those who consider themselves ultra-highly sophisticated. Profanity in particular, is an offense against God, against the third commandment—*"Thou shalt not take the name of the Lord thy God in vain,"* and against the sensitivity of any Christians who may hear.

If the foul things inside us would just stay quiet, things would not be so serious. However, they are persistently active, ever trying to get expression, to say something or do something, and they become stronger and more active by each expression. Solomon gives us some good advice in Ecclesiastes 5:6, *"Do not let your mouth cause your flesh to sin?"* Be careful; if you let loose the word, then you have let loose the feeling; but if you conquer the word, you have conquered the feeling.

OPPOSITES OUGHT NOT TO COME FROM THE SAME SOURCE.

> *"With it we bless our God and Father, and with it we curse men, who have been made in the similitude of God. Out of the same mouth proceed blessing and cursing. My brethren, these things ought not to be so."* (vs. 9, 10).

Human beings are a bundle of contradictions. Nothing, says James, illustrates these contradictions better than the tongue. Is it not remarkable that the same person may put the tongue to good and bad uses? At one moment, we use it to praise and worship the Lord; a little while later we use it to curse others who are made in the image of the God we profess to worship. If we bless God as our father, it should teach us to speak well of and to all who bear his image. The same mouth that can praise God ought not to be heard invoking curses upon persons. Inconsistency of speech breeds inconsistency of action.

An Indian pastor who was worried over the inconsistent lives among some of his flock said to a missionary, "There is much crooked walked by those who make good talk." It is sad when a Christian believes in Christ and acts like a devil. How inconsistent it is for the same mouth to bless the father and curse the children! The inconsistency appears on the very face of the English word "curse." To curse is the very reverse of "to bless." It bears the connotation of harm or catastrophe, and of judgment.

"These things ought not to be this way." They are oral inconsistencies! Inconsistency is displeasing to God since it is always his purpose that we always use our tongue to bless others and glorify him. He is ready and able, though the gift of the Holy spirit, to make it possible for us to do this. Only the supernatural power of God can enable us to control the perverse and wayward tongue. That is why the extent to which we can control our speech is an index of our submission to God. The more we are obeying the

Holy Spirit, the greater will be our ability to control ourselves in every area of life—including how we use our speech.

The tongue that blesses the Father, and then turns around and curses persons made in God's image, is in desperate need of spiritual medicine! If the tongue is inconsistent, there is something radically wrong with the heart; *these things ought not so to be.* They are oral inconsistencies! In the gospel of Matthew 15:18 we are told, *"But those things which proceed out of the mouth come from the heart, and they defile a man."* If evil lives in our heart, the tongue cannot help but to produce oral inconsistencies. If hate is in our heart, that is what fruit the tongue will produce. If jealousy is in your heart that is the kind of fruit the tongue will produce.

Our words can refresh and encourage someone that is discouraged and ready to give up and quit. Words can give new life to a dead relationship. The Greek definition for encourage is "one who puts courage IN the heart of another"

****

A Greek philosopher once asked his servant to prepare him the best dish he could. The servant prepared tongue. When asked why he considered this the best dish, he replied, "I have observed, sir, that the tongue can sing sweet melodies; it can engage in intelligent conversation, it can teach the ignorant, it can plead with the wayward, and it can speak compliments that brighten people's lives.

Sometime later, the philosopher asked his servant to prepare the worst dish he could think of. Again, he prepared tongue. "Why do you now say that this is the worst dish," asked the philosopher? "O master, the tongue can also tell viscous lies, spread terrible gossip, defame a person's character, destroy friendships, and bring discouragement." How right he was! [9]

How we use the gift of speech, then, is vitally important—to you, to those who hear you, and to God. Your use of the tongue reveals how you think and whether your life is God-centered or

---

[9] http://www.sermoncentral.com/Illustration/Tongue, Bill Butsko

self-centered. Your use of the gift of speech may determine whether the "good life" can be yours. "*Whoever would love life and see good days must keep his tongue from evil and his lips from deceitful speech*" (1 Peter 3:10, NIV).

Learning to live the "good life" is not just a matter of getting rid of, or taking off, or breaking off, or getting away from something. In actuality it is all those things but more so a matter of losing the desire for, because of spiritual maturity. In 1 Corinthians 13:11 Paul says, "*When I was a child, I spoke as a child, I understood as a child, I thought as a child; but when I became a man, I put away childish things.*"

As you mature in Christ there are some things, you have to put away.

- Some of the things I use to say I won't say now
- Some of what I use to do I won't do now
- Some of the things I use to think about I don't think about now

Christianity is not so much a series of "giving-ups" as it is a totally new life. As we come to know Christ better, we find that some things no longer interest us. As we mature in our faith in Christ, God adds so much to our lives that there is no room for the old things. The first thing we know, we have lost interest in the old and are busy with the new life in Christ. If you want to get the outward expression of your life in order, it begins with setting your heart towards God. Only when Jesus is truly the Lord of our life, only when we have sincerely submitted and allowed Him to sit on the throne of our heart, only when we have declared Him as our Savior can we begin to say things, as they ought to be said. God can use our tongues to direct others into a way of life and to delight them in the trials of life. The tongue is a little member, but it has great power. Give God your life, your tongue, and your heart each day and ask Him to use you to be a blessing to others.

REFLECTIONS AND MEDITATIONS

1. How aware are you that what you say reveals the thoughts of your heart?
2. How would applying T.H.I.N.K. before you speak affect your conversation with others?
3. Does your speech contradict with your claim of being a follower of Christ?

CHAPTER 8

"WISDOM THAT IS FROM ABOVE"

James 3:13-18

> *But the wisdom that is from above is first pure, then peaceable, gentle, willing to yield, full of mercy and good fruits, without partiality and without hypocrisy. (James 3:17)*

Much of secular education is concerned with helping people know what their teachers know. When one takes English, math, or gym what the teacher's character is of little or no importance. The goal is to learn as much as you can, get a good grade, and pass the class. It probably should not be that way but that is the way it is. On the other hand, Christian education is concerned with helping people become as their teachers are. A Christian teacher must be able to say, *"Be ye followers of me, as I also am of Christ"* (1 Corinthians 11:1, KJV).

All of us have heard of preachers and teachers who are knowledgeable and who may say good things, but who somehow miss the heart of God's message, and fail to relate truth to their everyday life. All of us know people who are very intelligent, perhaps almost geniuses, and yet who seemingly are unable to carry out the simplest task of life. They can speak well, comprehend the most difficult task, design, and run computers, but they have difficulty managing their own lives! Many highly trained and educated individuals although extremely intelligent, have trouble getting along in the simplest way with others. Their abundance of knowledge can often render them useless and abrasive.

It is this kind of "knowledge without wisdom" that James is writing about? In this passage, he is contrasting real wisdom, with false wisdom, that which is earthly, sensual, and devilish. How wise are you? What kind of wisdom do you have?

TRUE WISDOM IS REFLECTED IN ONE'S CONDUCT.

> *"Who is wise and understanding among you? Let him show by good conduct that his works are done in the meekness of wisdom."* (vs. 13)

Sometimes we confuse knowledge and wisdom. Knowledge is the possession of facts, information, or skills acquired through training or experience. Wisdom is superior to knowledge-it is skill in the use of knowledge. It is keen insight and the ability to judge soundly. A person with a good education may have knowledge but if they lack wisdom, they will find it hard to make good use of the facts they have learned. On the other hand, a person who has wisdom will be shrewd and discerning even though he or she lacks formal education. Sometimes we say such a person has 'what it takes,' that he has 'street sense,' that they know 'how to hustle," that they have "mother wit."

In a spiritual context, true wisdom is the ability to apply divine truth to daily life. True wisdom involves not only knowing the truth but also knowing how to use it. Some of us are 'Word' smart, but 'application' dumb. We can say all what the bible says, but have trouble putting it into practical everyday use. The mere possession of factual knowledge is no assurance that we can use it wisely. It is good to get into the Word, but it is better to get the Word into us. It is good to search the Scriptures, but we also need to let the Scriptures search us for problems that need to be fixed.

Wisdom, as used in the Bible, is based on respect and a personal trust in the Lord. *"The fear of the Lord is the beginning of wisdom, and the knowledge of the holy is understanding"* (Proverbs 9:10). A wise person recognizes their relationship to God. They acknowledge God's greatness, holiness, and majesty. They are aware that in themselves they cannot meet God's requirements for goodness and faithfulness. Their awareness of personal inability makes them humble before God, and their humility leads them to the sort of conduct God requires.

James speaks of good conduct meaning the total of one's lifestyle-or good behavior. A wise person is an obedient person, and change is a regular feature of their life. If we are going to be wise, a review of what has happened in the past, with an eye to do better in the future, is going to have to be a regular part of our lives. There must be a continual willingness to go back to the truth and change in conformity with God's truth.

James says a wise person lives his life in a spirit of meekness. When we talk about meekness, some people automatically relate meekness with weakness. Meekness is not weakness; it is power under control. The Greek word used is for a horse that had been broken so that it power was under control. A stallion is not weak because he has submitted to a bit in his mouth and a rider on his back. His power has only been channeled productively. The meek person seeks only the glory of God and does not cater to the praises of persons. Meekness is the fruit of the spirit; we cannot manufacture it. Meekness is the right use of power, and wisdom is the right use of knowledge. They go together. The truly wise person will show in his daily life that he is a child of God. Attitude and action go together.

True wisdom is bound up with the life of faith in Jesus Christ. *"From childhood you have known the Holy Scriptures, which are able to make you wise for salvation through faith which is in Christ Jesus"* (2 Tim 3:15). True wisdom is God's gift. It is not gained by conversing with people, nor by the knowledge of the world (as some think and speak), but it comes from the above. If you lack knowledge, go to school. If you lack wisdom, get on your knees!

Knowledge is not wisdom. Wisdom is the proper use of knowledge. True wisdom will issue forth in a life of meekness, a life that has power under control.

A wise person, in God's sight, is not necessarily a person who has earned a graduate degree. Rather, a wise person is a believer in Christ Jesus who lives according to God's will. If you want to impress God, if you want really to be someone, get an advanced degree. Get a doctorate in love, in obedience, and in doing the truth. How wise are you? What kind of wisdom do you have? If you have true wisdom, it will be reflected in your conduct.

COUNTERFEIT WISDOM PRODUCES LACK OF HUMILITY.

> *"But if you have bitter envy and self-seeking in your hearts, do not boast and lie against the truth. This wisdom does not descend from above, but is earthly, sensual, demonic. For where envy and self-seeking exist, confusion and every evil thing are there."* (vs. 14-16)

What is the origin of human wisdom? James tells us the believer has three enemies: the world, the flesh, and the devil. These enemies are suggested by the terms: earthly, sensual, and demonic.

The devil has an imitation, a substitute product for almost everything God gives us. He has wisdom that will confound and confuse us if we do not have the wisdom of God. His brand of wisdom is earthy; it is the wisdom of this world. It is natural as opposed to spiritual. This wisdom gets its origin in human nature totally apart from the Spirit of God. It is devilish, or demonic, in that it originates with the devil rather than with God. It leads to arrogance, smugness, feelings of superiority, self-sufficiency, abandonment of God's morality and authority, lack of trustfulness, selfish ambition, bitter jealousy, and humanistic philosophies to God's word.

The true wisdom comes from above, but the false wisdom comes from below. In other words, there is "heavenly wisdom" that comes from God, and there is "humanly made wisdom" that does not come from God. Whatever does not come from God is destined to fail. No matter how successful it may seem to be at the time.

- The Scriptures tell us that human wisdom is foolishness to God. *"Where is the wise? Where is the scribe? Where is the disputer of this age? Has not God made foolish the wisdom of this world?"* (1 Corinthians 1:20),
- The Scriptures tell us that God's wisdom is foolishness to humans. *"But the natural man does not receive the things of the Spirit of God, for they are foolishness to him; nor can he know them, because they are spiritually discerned."* (1 Corinthians 2:14).
- The Scriptures tell us that human worldly wisdom will come to nothing. *"For it is written: "I will destroy the wisdom of the wise, and bring to nothing the understanding of the prudent"* (1 Corinthians 1:19), while God's wisdom will endure forever.

Because the world has turned from God, it has lost its wisdom. Every increase in human knowledge only magnifies the problems. What are the evidences of false wisdom? James says they are "envy and self-seeking."

Dr. Charles Swindoll says, "There are twins within the soul that are evil: envy and jealousy. Though they seem similar, they are quite different.

- Envy is felt when we mourn empty hands because we don't have what someone else has
- Jealousy is felt when we have full hands and are threatened because we fear someone will take away what we have
- Envy begins with nothing
- Jealousy begins with much

Where there is envy and jealousy, it excites strife. Strife promotes rivalry and division and endeavors to excuse itself by boasting and lying; and immediately thereafter follows confusion. Confusion then sets the stage for "every evil work." How wise are you? What kind of wisdom do you have? If you have true wisdom, it will be reflected in the works that you do.

HEAVENLY WISDOM LEADS TO PEACE.

> *"But the wisdom that is from above is first pure, then peaceable, gentle, willing to yield, full of mercy and good fruits, without partiality and without hypocrisy. Now the fruit of righteousness is sown in peace by those who make peace"* (vs. 17, 18).

The wisdom that is from above, God's wisdom, operates in a different way from the wisdom that is "earthy, sensual, and demonic."

What is the Christian's wisdom? Do we look to the philosophies of this world? No! To begin with, Jesus Christ is our wisdom. In Jesus Christ are hid all the treasures of wisdom and knowledge. The first step toward true wisdom is the receiving of Jesus Christ as Savior. It is not only having knowledge of him, but the acknowledgement of him as your Savior, as your Lord, as your redeemer, as your helper.

James presents heavenly wisdom as possessed of seven great characteristics. Seven was the perfect number among the Jews. There are seven notes in the harmony of Christian character; or seven colors in the rainbow of the Christian Life, which, when blended, form its pure white sunlight. Of these seven, the first is marked off from the others, because it refers to what a person is within their own heart, while the other six deal with the qualities shown by true wisdom accompanying one's attitude and action toward other people.

A Christian must first be **pure**. Purity is the fundamental characteristic of everything that is from above. God is holy; therefore, the wisdom from above is pure. Righteousness lies at the foundation of all that is beautiful in character. Christian wisdom leads a person *"to keep himself unspotted from the world."* God's wisdom leads to purity of life. Humanity's wisdom leads to sin. Wisdom's chief element is holiness. That purity is obtained through the blood of Jesus Christ and by the indwelling of the Spirit.

Then peaceable—Man's wisdom leads to competition, rivalry, and war; but God's wisdom leads to peace. It is a peace based on holiness, not on compromise. God never has "peace at any price." There ought to be peace in the church. However, the peace of the church is not more important than the purity of the church. The church can never have peace by sweeping sins under the rug and pretending they are not there. Human wisdom says, "Cover up sin! Keep things together!" God's wisdom says, "Confess sin and my peace will keep things together." If the church is pure, devoted to God, then there will be peace.

Gentle—the gentle person does not deliberately cause fights, but neither do they compromise the truth to keep the peace. In Plato's era, the term gentle was used to describe a brilliant teacher who could dialogue with his student without getting angry. It was a word meaning, "to be under control."

Willing to yield—or easy to get along with. The accommodating person is willing to hear all sides of a question, but he or she does not compromise their convictions. He or she can disagree without being disagreeable.

Full of mercy and good fruits—the person who follows God's wisdom is controlled by mercy, a willingness to forgive. God's wisdom does not make a life empty; it makes it full. God's wisdom is practical; it changes the life and produces good works to the glory of God.

Without partiality—when we lean on the world's wisdom, we are pressured from one side then the other to change our mind or take another viewpoint. When we have God's wisdom, we need not waver. We can be decisive and not be afraid. Wisdom for above brings strength from above.

Finally, **without hypocrisy**—when humanity's wisdom is at work, there must be genuine sincerity. When God's wisdom is at work, there is openness and honesty in people "speaking the truth in love."

- What we are is what we live
- What we live is the result of what we plant
- What we plant determines what we reap
- If we live in **God's wisdom**, we plant righteousness and peace, and we reap God's blessing
- If we live in **human worldly wisdom**, we plant sin and war and we reap "confusion and every evil work"

Proverbs 3:13 declares, *"Happy is the man who finds wisdom, and the man who gains understanding."* How wise are you? What kind of wisdom do you have? If you have true wisdom, you will manifest certain characteristics. The origin of true spiritual wisdom is of God. To get your wisdom from any other source is to ask for trouble. There is no need to get the counterfeit wisdom of the world, the wisdom that caters to the flesh and accompanies the work of the devil. Get your wisdom from God.

****

A certain psychotic was convinced that he was dead, so he was committed to the care of a psychiatrist to cure him. The psychiatrist had the man read an anatomy book and watch the films to show him that dead men do not bleed. Then, he took him to a room full of cadavers, where the man saw for himself that dead men do not bleed. "All right, I'm convinced; dead men do not bleed." The doctor then took a pin and poked the man; a tiny drop of blood appeared on the man's finger. "Well, what do you know," he responded. "Dead men do bleed after all."

There are always those who have arrived at their own. They are not going to change no matter what you say, do, or what they see. They have their own wisdom and nothing is going to make them change. Some people will deny the truth no matter what the evidence is.

You may have heard the message of the cross preached in every conceivable way. Jesus has been preached as the Suffering Servant who died on the cross for your sins. He has been preached as the Lord and Savior of your life. He has been preached as the Son of God who has gone to prepare a place for you in heaven. Yet, you still operate according to the wisdom of the world. Opposite of the man who thought he was dead, you think you are alive. The wisdom of the Bible declares that if you do not know Jesus, you are *"dead in trespasses and sins"* (Ephesians 2:1). You may look good, but you are dead. The wisdom of the Bible declares in Roman 3:23, *"for all have sinned and fall short of the glory of God."* And in Romans 6:23 it declares, *"For the wages of sin is death, but the gift of God is eternal life in Christ Jesus our Lord."* What will it take to convince you today? How wise are you? What kind of wisdom do you have? True wisdom is from above and declares *"the fruit of the Spirit is love, joy, peace, longsuffering, kindness, goodness, faithfulness, gentleness, self-control" (*Galatians 5:22).

REFLECTIONS AND MEDITATIONS

1. Does your conduct and your speech reflect that you are a wise person?
2. What is the source of your wisdom?
3. How are the seven characteristics of heavenly wisdom manifested when you find yourself in a controversial situation?

CHAPTER 9

"MOVING TOWARDS HARMONY AND HOLINESS"

James 4:1-12

"Therefore submit to God. Resist the devil and he will flee from you. Draw near to God and He will draw near to you. Cleanse your hands, you sinners; and purify your hearts, you double-minded. Lament and mourn and weep! Let your laughter be turned to mourning and your joy to gloom. Humble yourselves in the sight of the Lord, and He will lift you up." (James 4:7-10)

A man named Stephen Brown explains that when a group of thoroughbred horses faces attack, they stand in a circle facing each other and with their back legs kick out at the enemy. On the other hand, donkeys may be observed to do just the opposite; they face the enemy and kick each other! I am not an expert on either horses or donkeys but what he says does give way to thoughts about the church.

When we consider the church, how do we respond to threats and attacks among our community of believers? We might not like to admit it but we often respond to troubles in our ranks more like donkeys than thoroughbreds. We ignore the real enemy and attack fellow believers. We often kick, bite, and snap at each other rather than at the real enemy. As much as we would like it to be, the church is not exempt from troubles, disagreements, and controversies. Like it or not we all have come out of the world and some of us are not quite as sanctified, are not as set apart and separated from our old ways, as we will ultimately be.

In the passage before us James acknowledges that there are problems in the community of believers, the church, as he asks the question, "*Where do wars and fights come from among you?*" He then answers his own question, "*Do they not come from your desires for pleasure that war in your members?*" As the church grows the addition of more and more people, brings more attitudes, more people who are at different levels of spiritual understanding, the potential for more and more conflict, and the potential for more wars and fights among us. How are we in the midst of a growing church to keep the church moving towards harmony and holiness? How are we to keep ourselves focused on who the real enemy is, and not on attacking each other? The first thing we need to do is acknowledge. . .

THE SOURCE OF CONFLICTS.

A. An overwhelming desire to satisfy self.

> *"Where do wars and fights come from among you? Do they not come from your desires for pleasure that war in your members? You lust and do not have. You murder and covet and cannot obtain. You fight and war. Yet you do not have because you do not ask. You ask and do not receive, because you ask amiss, that you may spend it on your pleasures"* (vs. 1-3)

Within each of us, there is an ongoing war. Most of us are not content with the issues of life. We have desires for success, desires to have this or that. Desires to become more than what we are and sometimes these desires can be so overwhelming that they manifest themselves outwardly in some ugly attitudes, jealousy, envy, and a host of other evil ways. James says that our lusts and desires can even rise to the level of murder. None of us would like to think that we are capable of murder behind the desire to possess something, but we see it happening each day. Although we may not commit the physical act, we can daily slay and make victims of those around us. As we learned in chapter 7, we can assassinate people with our tongues.

Interestingly, James attributes the source of fighting and wars not to our being denied by others what we desire to have, but to our inability to obtain what we need from God. His counsel is two-fold. One, we "*do not have because we do not ask.*" And two, if we do ask, we ask wrongly, *"You ask and do not receive, because you ask amiss, that you may spend it on your pleasures."*

In Matthew 7:7-11 Jesus made it very clear to his disciples that it is God's desire to provide for his children when they ask. Jesus indicated that prayer is a progressive work, that if pursued will yield results. *"Ask, and it will be given to you; seek, and you will find; knock, and it will be opened to you. "For everyone who asks receives, and he who seeks finds, and to him who knocks it will be opened. "Or what man is there among you who, if his son asks for bread, will give him a stone? "Or if he asks for a fish, will he give him a serpent? "If you then, being evil, know how to give good gifts to your children, how much more will your Father who is in heaven give good things to those who ask Him!"* We do not have what we want because we do not ask God.

On the other hand, many of us would say that we regularly ask of God for things, in prayer. Even if we ask, we must recognize, however, that God will not grant us every request we make. It would be disastrous to us if God granted us our every wish. Some of us are where we are today because God said no, or put us on hold. Sometimes He delays his answer, giving us time to get ready to receive it, to learn patience, or to recognize that we don't really need what we asked for. Some of us have met someone and asked God to give us a relationship with that person only to find out that they were a scoundrel and we praised God that he did not answer our prayer.

Some, says James, do ask, but their petitions go unanswered because they ask amiss (literally, "with an evil intent.") They ask for the wrong reason, and God does not answer their prayers. They pray selfishly for things to satisfy their own lusts.

B. Our affections often cause us to violate our relationship with God. James expresses it this way:

> *"Adulterers and adulteresses! Do you not know that friendship with the world is enmity with God? Whoever therefore wants to be a friend of the world makes himself an enemy of God. . . Therefore He says: "God resists the proud, but gives grace to the humble."* (vs. 4, 6b)

In the Old Testament, God's relationship to the Israelites was sometimes depicted as a marriage. Israel's unfaithfulness to God was then described as adultery. We are in a covenant relationship with God just as we are in marriage with our spouses. It is a relationship based on faithfulness and trust. Marriage is between one man and one woman freely and totally committed to each other as companions for life. The marriage covenant, the marriage bond, is broken and the relationship violated when a third party is allowed to enter in. That marital partner then becomes an adulterer or adulteress.

A Christian who divides their allegiance between God and the world is like an unfaithful spouse, because lack of loyalty to God and Christ constitute spiritual adultery. One cannot be a friend to the world without being the enemy of God. Those who seek friendship with the world, who want to copulate with the physical and material gods of the world, are in effect committing 'spiritual adultery' and making themselves enemies of God. Claiming to be in a covenant relationship with God while at the same time chasing after and pursuing the things of the world is committing spiritual adultery. It displays a prideful and arrogant attitude in the very face of God. God declares in Isaiah 13:11 (NIV), *"I will punish the world for its evil, the wicked for their sins. I will put an end to the arrogance of the haughty and will humble the pride of the ruthless."*

James declares, *"God resists the proud, but gives grace to the humble."* That is, he shows favor to the humble. The humble receive this favor because they recognize their shortcomings and faults and place themselves in a position to receive God's blessings. Only those with a contrite heart can come to him. Psalm 51:17 declares, *"The sacrifices of God are a broken spirit, a broken and a contrite heart--these, O God, you will not despise."*

If we are to keep the church moving towards harmony and holiness we must first recognize self-satisfaction, pride and arrogance, set us at odds with God. The second thing we need to do is . . .

REPENT AND CHANGE OUR ATTITUDES.

> *"Therefore submit to God. Resist the devil and he will flee from you. Draw near to God and He will draw near to you. Cleanse your hands, you sinners; and purify your hearts, you double-minded. Lament and mourn and weep! Let your laughter be turned to mourning and your joy to gloom. Humble yourselves in the sight of the Lord, and He will lift you up."* (vs. 7-10)

James tells us if we are to move towards harmony and holiness, we must repent of the sin of lustful selfish desires and humble ourselves before God. In these three verses, he gives us ten commands regarding how we can move towards harmony and holiness. James tells us to: submit, resist, draw near, cleanse, purify, lament, mourn, weep, turn our laughter into mourning, and to humble ourselves.

James tells us to first ***submit** to God.* "Submit" is a military term meaning "to be subordinated" or "to render obedience." He then tells us second, to resist the devil. **Resist** means to "take a stand against." Take a stand against the devil, *and he will flee.*

Resisting the devil means recognizing Satan's presence, intentions, power—, and refusing to yield to his tempting. When temptation comes, remember that you do not have to give in (1 Corinthians 10:13).

In resisting Satan we must do it boldly, using the Scriptures as our weapon and relying upon God to give us strength. It is not wise to try to argue with him for he is the master of clever argument. We need to follow the example of Jesus who turned away the devil by quoting Scripture (Matthew 4:1-11). At the same time, we need to note that Jesus' one encounter with Satan did not permanently keep him away. Luke 4:13 tells us that Satan *"departed from him for a season,"* clearly implying that he came back later to tempt Jesus again.

Instead of succumbing to Satan's desire to separate us from God we should, third, **draw near** to him. James tells not only to resist the devil, but to *draw near to God and he will draw near to you.* Drawing near to God involves something more than merely praying. It calls for a deep, full surrender to him—a letting go of anything that comes between you and him, a walking closely with him. If you draw near to God, you quit fighting his plan for you, you put yourself at his disposal, and you accept without question whatever he sends. You find your greatest joy in doing his will. Drawing near to God is the ultimate expression of the life of faith, of complete dependence on the Lord; it will result in God's drawing near to you in a richly satisfying spiritual experience.

You cannot very well resist the devil and draw near to God without proper preparation (v. 8b). To draw near to God demands two things, this numbers four and five. *Cleanse your hands, you sinners; and purify your hearts, you double-minded.* Both "*cleanse*" and "*purify*" are verbs that refer to ceremonial cleansing. The need for cleansing is clear from the way James addressed his readers, "you sinners" and "you double-minded" (vs. 8, 9)

If there is sin on our hands, and in our hearts, we need the cleansing of confession and forgiveness. A double-minded person is one who vacillates between God and the world, unable to take a firm stand with either. To allow the devil to entice us away from a single-minded allegiance to God is to become divided in our loyalties, 'double-minded' and spiritually unstable. What is required then is repentance from both this external behavior (cleanse your hands) and this internal attitude (purify your hearts). The Psalmist required *'clean hands and a pure heart'* for those who would stand before the Lord (Psalm 24:3-4); James asks the same of those who would *'draw near to God.'* With the help of the Holy Spirit, we must make up our minds, once for all, to give God our way. If we are double-minded and not sure whether we are living for God or for the world, our hearts must be purified and unified.

James issues a call for his readers to abandon their worldly foolishness as they turn to God. He tells us, in verses 6-9, to ***lament*** *and* ***mourn*** *and* ***weep****! Let your laughter be* ***turned*** *to mourning and your joy to gloom.* He is not demanding that Christians' lives should be devoid of all joy. What he is requiring is that persons who have allowed their lives to become entangled in the silly pursuits of worldly pleasures, and refuse to take sin seriously, should realize the danger of judgement in the world to come.

Finally ten, James says, ***"Humble*** *yourselves in the sight of the Lord, and He will lift you up."* The people of James' day, when they wanted to express contrition, would roll in the dust until the one whom they had offended pardoned them. We need not do that if we humble ourselves and express our sorrow at sin to God. How is it then that we are to humble ourselves in the sight of God? First, to humble oneself is not to say, "I'm nothing." Rather, it is to recognize one's own proper relationship to God their Creator. The humble person does not think too highly nor too lowly of himself or herself. They accept their strengths and weaknesses and serve God and humanity to the best of their ability without calling attention to themselves.

How are we in the midst of a growing church to keep the church moving towards harmony and holiness? We must humble ourselves before the Lord, recognize our spiritual poverty, acknowledge our desperate need of God's help, and submit to his commanding will for all our lives.

****

Mr. Smith and Mr. Jones were in a rather severe disagreement over a very trivial matter. This deeply concerned Deacon Brown, so he prayed that he might be a peacemaker.

Deacon Brown called on Smith and asked, "What do you think of Jones?" "He's the biggest grump in the neighborhood!" "But," said Deacon Brown, "You have to admit that Jones is very kind to his family." "Oh, sure, Jones is kind to his family all right; no one can deny that."

The next day Deacon Brown went to Jones and inquired, "Do you know what Smith said about you?" "No, but I can imagine how that rascal would lie about me!" "This may surprise you, but Smith said you're very kind to your family." "What! Did Smith say that?" "Yes, he did." "Well, if you hadn't told me, I wouldn't believe it." "What do you think of Smith?" asked Deacon Brown. "Truthfully, I believe he's a lowdown scalawag." "But you have to admit that he's very honest in business." "Yes, there's no getting around that; in business he's a man you can trust."

The next day, Deacon Brown called on Smith again. "You know what Jones said about you? He claims you're a fellow that really can be trusted in business, and that you're perfectly honest." "You mean it?" "Yes, I do," said Deacon Brown. "Well of all things," replied Smith with a happy smile.

The next Sunday the former "enemies" nodded to each other. Deacon Brown continued his "holy meddling" until the next annual business meeting of the church when Smith and Jones shook hands and finally voted on the same side![10]

How are we to keep the church moving towards harmony and holiness? Anyone can help to propagate gossip and conflict. It takes a loving person to see the good in others. We must recognize that the job of Christians is to help resolve conflict, not start more of it. The job of Christians is to not become wrapped up and consumed in selfish desires that hinder our prayers and render us spiritually

---

10 http://www.sermoncentral.com/illustrations/sermon-illustration-alison-bucklin-stories-peace-79169.asp

impotent. The job of Christians is to recognize who the real enemy is, the devil, and to resist him by having right standing with God.

Here are some simple and practical suggestions that will help you move towards harmony and holiness:

- When arguing with a stupid person, be sure he/she isn't doing the same thing
- When one will not, two cannot quarrel
- A quarrel is like buttermilk, the longer it stands the more sour it becomes
- Perhaps the only way to avoid quarreling with your wife is to let her go her way and you go hers

The most important however is this one: We must be in tune with Christ to be in harmony with one another.

How are we to keep the church moving towards harmony and holiness? We must all be in tune with Christ, that is, we must be holy, saved, and sanctified, before we can be in harmony with each other.

- If there is going to be harmony and holiness in your home
- If there is going to be harmony and holiness on your job
- If there is going to be harmony and holiness in your life

It all begins with being in harmony with Christ. You cannot be in harmony with anyone until you are in harmony with Christ.

REFLECTIONS AND MEDITATIONS

1. Can you recognize the source of conflict with those whom you have disagreements?
2. Are there areas of your life contrary to God's Word of which you need to repent?
3. Are you one who is promoting harmony and holiness within the body of Christ?

CHAPTER 10

"DON'T BE TOO CONFIDENT ABOUT THE FUTURE!"

James 4:13-17

The centerpiece of Christian planning ought to be the acknowledgment of God's sovereign will.

"Instead you ought to say, "If the Lord wills, we shall live and do this or that." (James 4:15)

Legend has it that a certain college philosophy professor asked one question on his final exam. He picked up a chair, put it on his desk, and wrote on the board, "Using everything we have learned this semester, prove that this chair does not exist." The students dug deep and wrote like crazy for a whole hour, some of them churning out 30 pages of heady philosophical debate and logic. However, one student turned in his paper after less than a minute. Turned out he was the only one to get an "A." What did he write so quickly that turned out to be just the right answer? "What chair?"

What would you write about if someone asked you to prove there is no tomorrow? The simplest answer is probably, "What tomorrow?" No one has ever seen tomorrow. Tomorrow is a day that never comes for when we experience the day we can only talk of it as today. Tomorrow is just a yesterday that has not arrived yet.

- Kay Lyons said, "Yesterday is a canceled check; tomorrow is a promissory note; today is the only cash you have--so spend it wisely."
- Henry Ward Beecher said, "Every tomorrow has two handles; we can take hold of the handle of anxiety or the handle of faith."

Some of us plan our lives as if without a doubt our lives will go on from day to day. With great assurance, we talk of tomorrow. We live as if all of our plans for the future will succeed. Many people live each day as if it were promised, as if they are in charge of all the circumstances of their fate. In reality, we propose, but God is the one who decides. The centerpiece of Christian planning ought to be the acknowledgment of God's sovereign will. We plan, but God allows. Today we need to pause and ask ourselves where God figures in our plans for the future.

CHRISTIANS OFTEN PLAN WITH A SPIRIT OF SELF-RELIANCE.

> *Come now, you who say, "Today or tomorrow we will go to such and such a city, spend a year there, buy and sell, and make a profit"; whereas you do not know what will happen tomorrow. For what is your life? It is even a vapor that appears for a little time and then vanishes away.* (vs. 13, 14)

In this verse, James concisely sums up the attitude of those whose lives are caught in the concerns of the world. The persons of James text are typical businesspeople who make their plans apart from God. They are self-assertive in their travel plans: *we will go to such and such a city,* self-confident of their time schedule, *spend a year there*; and self-centered in their trade relationships, *buy and sell, and make a profit.* James paints a vivid picture of the Jewish merchant, an enterprising salesperson out drumming up business for the bottom-line purpose of making money. James is not disapproving of their ambition, their planning, or their hard work. What he disapproves of is that they order their lives as if they were in complete control—as if God had no place in their plans. To these self-centered hustlers James simply states, "Why, *you do not know what will happen tomorrow.*"

The story is told of a man who stopped to chat with a farmer who was erecting a new building. He asked, "What are you putting up?" The farmer replied, "Well, if I can rent it, it's a rustic cottage. If I can't rent it, it's a cow shed. That farmer is one who, unlike these merchants, recognized that his plans were tentative. He could propose, but reality could prove otherwise.

In response to their self-centered attitude, James pointedly asks: *What is your life?* The answer is *a* vapor ("a *mist*, a puff of steam."). James compares life to a vapor, an effective figure depicting human frailty. Human life is like the morning mist that covers the mountain that fades away at the rising of the sun. We form plans about our business and family affairs, plans about our jobs and homes, plans to improve our social status; and we often forget that all these are dependent upon an unknown quantity—our continuance in life and health, of which only God is totally in control.

None of us knows for sure what tomorrow will bring; let alone a year from now. We sometimes hear this verse read at funerals. It is certainly appropriate there, but we ought to be reminded of it daily. It is not the mere looking forward that is forbidden, but the looking forward without the recollection that while "people propose, it is God who decides."

We should note that James does not attack business as evil in itself nor does he deny that trades-people and merchants may be pious and God-fearing persons. He does not even assert that there is anything sinful in the desire to get gain. What he reproves is so complete an absorption in the affairs of the world that God is forgotten. Where does God figure in our plans for the future? With what attitude do we consider tomorrow?

THE CENTERPIECE OF CHRISTIAN PLANNING OUGHT TO BE THE ACKNOWLEDGMENT OF GOD'S SOVEREIGN WILL.

> *Instead you ought to say, "If the Lord wills, we shall live and do this or that." But now you boast in your arrogance. All such boasting is evil.* (vs. 15, 16)

In this passage, those who make their plans without considering God are what we might call practical atheists. There are various kinds of atheists:

Those who openly deny God's existence—pure atheists
Those who do not know if He exists—agnostics
Those who live as if He did not exist—practical atheists

This latter type is by far the largest group. They probably would not consider themselves atheists as commonly defined; and if you asked, they probably would say they believed in God—at least in some kind of god.[11] With their lips, they may affirm a faith in God, but they continue to live as if God does not exist, or at least does not matter.

The presumptuous pride displayed by the self-sufficient person is arrogant, evil, and sinful. It is arrogant because it exalts the person. It is also evil and sinful because it ignores God. This kind of boasting is especially foolish because in one brief moment an incident beyond one's control can occur that may alter drastically the whole course of life.

Many people in seemingly good health fell sick on yesterday. In a matter of seconds, their lives were changed forever. Many, if not all, had plans for the future. If we had asked, they would have told us of plans to go here or there, and do this or that, to buy a new car, a new home, attend a wedding, but all those plans in a few vital

---

11 William J. Krutza and Philip P. Di Cicco, *Living That Counts: A Study Guide to the book of James* (Grand Rapids, MI: Baker House, 1974), 88.

seconds were changed. Proverbs 27:1 rightly declares, "*Do not boast about tomorrow, for you do not know what a day may bring forth.*"

The key to avoiding boasting is to maintain a godly perspective. Instead of making big plans on a human plane, we must expand our view to include God in the picture. In place of vain boasting we should say, "*If it is the Lord's will, we will live and do this or that.*" How does James intend for us to use these words? These are not words to be used like some charm to be added as an addendum to every prayer, or to follow everything that we say regarding the future. Instead, James intends for us to have a realistic attitude of heart that affects all our being and behavior.

Dr. Martin Luther King once said as he considered the present and looked into the future, "Like anybody I would like to live a long life. Longevity has its place. But I'm not concerned about that now. I just want to do God's will. And he's allowed me to go up to the mountain. I've looked over, and I've seen the Promised Land." [12] God has a will for each of us and in spite of how we plan it will be fulfilled; we need to be concerned about the present. Like Dr. King, we ought to be concerned with now doing God's will.

It is ungodly not to include the will of God in all our calculations, and to neglect to qualify our plans by a reference to that will. It is wicked for a finite and sinful person to map out the future of our lives acting as if the keys of time were in our own keeping, as if we could ensure life and health, like papers lockup in a fire-resistant safe. All such planning involves an arrogance that has in it the essence of all sin.

We all make some plans for tomorrow. To make those plans we must have certain expectations about what conditions may be tomorrow. Previous experience gives us confidence to believe that day will follow night, night will follow day, and that certain opportunities will probably be available for us. As long as we factor in the element of uncertainty, we are kept from presumption. We must humbly admit that we cannot control all circumstances. Only God has the power over all the contingencies that will determine

---

12 Martin Luther King, Jr.-1929-1968

whether our plans happen or not. We can expect our plans to succeed only if that is what he wants. We can propose but God has the power to dispose.

Well, maybe you are saying that is not me! I include God in everything I do. His will is the centerpiece of all of my plans. That being true, I pose to you the question, what are you planning?

GOD'S WILL IS FOR US IS TO ALWAYS PLAN TO DO GOOD.

> *Therefore, to him who knows to do good and does not do it, to him it is sin.* (vs. 17)

James makes a strange and interesting summary of what he has just said. The principle stated in this verse has its immediate application to the situation James has just discussed. Persons who order their lives without any reference to God are wrong. Since James has just informed his readers of this fact, those who ignore it are boastful, arrogant, and guilty of sin, but it also has broader applications. We are quick to recognize and condemn the overt sins of self-reliance, arrogance, murder, lying, stealing, and adultery, especially if they are not our sins. Many times, however, we fail to note what are commonly called the sins of omission—the good deed we did not do, the kind word we did not speak. James makes it clear that such neglect is sin also.

Many people claim comfort in saying, "I never did anybody any harm." To have not done harm is a good thing, but failing to do good is not. God desire for all of us is not merely that we should "cease to do evil," but also that we should learn to do good;" for "*to him who knows to do good and does not do it, to him it is sin.*" It is not only sin to do wrong; it is also sin to lose an opportunity of doing good. God means us not only to be harmless, but also to be useful; not only to be innocent, but to be followers of that which is good.

Some of us plan and include God's will, saying, *"If the Lord wills, we shall live and do this or that,"* but we still have as our goal a self-centered emphasis like these merchants. It has been said many people pray, not to find God's will, but to get his approval of their own. The pattern of Scripture is that we submit ourselves to God and we wait until God shows us what he is about to do. Or, we watch and see what God is doing around us and join him. God is the initiator. We adjust our lives to God so he can do through us what he wants to do. God is not our servant to adjust our plans. We are his servants, and we adjust our lives to what he is about to do. We never find God asking persons to dream up what they want to do for him. We do not sit down and dream what we want to do for God and then call God in to help us to accomplish it. Each of us needs to know what God has on his agenda for our lives, family, church, community, and our nation at this time in history. Then we can adjust our lives to God, so that he can move us into the mainstream of his activity. The focus needs to be on God's will, God's activity, and then knowing his will, we can then adjust our lives.

Some in our churches are not doing any harm, but neither are they doing any good. Their being there is not for the better or for the worse. When God convicts us of the good we need to do, *to him/her who knows to do good and does not do it, to him it is sin.*

****

A gray-haired pastor tells this story. "When my son was small, we often walked together out through the fields and neighboring pasture behind the parsonage. At first, the little fellow would hold onto my little finger, but he found that when he stepped into a hoof-print or stumbled over something, his grip would fail and down he'd go in the dust or snow. Not giving it much thought, my mind on other matters, I'd stop and he'd get up, brush himself off, and grab my little finger again, gripping a little harder this time.

"Needless to say, this occurred frequently until one day as he was brushing himself off, he looked at me and said, 'Daddy?' I replied, 'Yes, Son, what is it?' He said, I think if you would hold my hand, I wouldn't fall.' With a tear in his eye the pastor said, "You know, he still stumbled many times after that, but he never hit the ground."

The songwriter wrote. . . As you walk with God, don't try to hold on to Him, let Him hold on to you. You may stumble but He'll never let you fall."

People today are more troubled by gnawing doubts and agonizing fears than perhaps at any other time in history. James tells us what has gone wrong. We have planned our lives as if God did not exist, or at least as if he does, he does not matter. In trying to be masters of our fate, we have set our course and are confidently moving into the future. However, there is hope. That hope lies in humbly recognizing that we must restore God to His rightful place in our lives. Every plan we make ought to begin and end with, a conscious acknowledgment in our heart, if not on our lips, that whatever we plan to do we must always declare, *"If the Lord will."* The centerpiece of Christian planning ought to be the acknowledgment of God's sovereign will.

As you plan your future, I leave you with this consideration. The most dangerous of all delusions is that there is plenty of time. The most dangerous day in a person's life is when they learn there is such a word as tomorrow. There are things that must not be put off, because no person knows if tomorrow will ever come. Tomorrow is not promised. All you really have is right now. Many people are putting off giving their life to Christ, joining the church, and becoming involved. Many like the merchants say, *"Today or tomorrow we will go to such and such a city, spend a year there, buy and sell, and make a profit."* James statement and question to them then, and my question to you now is, "*you do not know what will happen tomorrow. For what is your life? It is even a vapor that appears for a little time and then vanishes away.* Don't be too confident about the future! Tomorrow is not promised.

- Tomorrow will be a better day if we begin today to improve it
- The best reason for doing the right thing today is tomorrow
- Learn from yesterday--live for today--hope for tomorrow

REFLECTIONS AND MEDITATIONS

1. Are you tentative in declaring your plans recognizing them all to be subject to the will of God?
2. How do you live a positive life in light of uncertainty all day?
3. Have you ever considered your sins of omission (things you have failed to do, turned away from, chosen to ignore)?

CHAPTER 11

"THE MISERY OF WEALTH"

James 5:1-6

Invest your wealth in the things that will truly give you peace and security for eternity.

Come now, you rich, weep and howl for your miseries that are coming upon you! (James 5:1)

Back in August of 2000, the Oprah Winfrey show. On that program, she had various people who were wealthy, including herself, that were sharing their stories of how wealth had changed their life. Some were wealthy through business ventures, some through dotcom stock, some had won the lottery. Most of them made remarks about how they were happier in their relationships with other people before they became wealthy. They complained of how wealth changed the people around them and how they were perceived more as money banks than persons were. However, although there was an element of frustration, disgust, and the feeling of being used none of them declared they wanted to give away what they had.

As I watched billionaire, Oprah cry and bemoan the fact that she was thought of by friends and family as only a money bank. She shared of the supposed emergency call from a family member that turned out to be a request for a new Mercedes Benz. I found it difficult to be compassionate for someone who has a billion dollars, more money than anyone could spend in a lifetime. As I thought about these people, it came to my mind that there would seem to be a contradiction between what James says to the rich "*weep and howl for your miseries that are coming upon you* and our normal perception of wealth. This is what we would call an oxymoron, where contradictory terms are often brought together in a phrase. Somehow, we seem to think that those who have wealth are exempt from misery, or if they encounter misery, they can still afford to do something about it. Given the choice, most of us would rather be miserable with a million dollars than without it. Amen!

In this passage, James brings three indictments against those who are rich. Three indictments that we may find it hard to relate to but that we should not dismiss. We may be inclined to think that these six verses apply only to people with huge fortunes. However, many of the men and women about whom James wrote in this passage were no better off than the majority of modern believers. Most of us would be classified as rich in comparison to believers in the first century church. Compared to the rest of the world, those of us who live in America are extremely rich, especially by comparison to those in third world countries. James is dealing not so much with the amount we might have, but with our attitudes toward money. What is your attitude toward your wealth? Your money?

The poor among the Jews received the gospel, and many of them believed; but generally, the rich rejected Christianity, and were hardened in their unbelief, hated, and persecuted those who believed on Christ. To these oppressing, unbelieving, persecuting, rich people, the apostle addresses himself in these six verses.

THE TANGIBLE THINGS OF THIS WORLD ARE CORRUPTIBLE.

> *Come now, you rich, weep and howl for your miseries that are coming upon you! Your riches are corrupted, and your garments are moth-eaten. Your gold and*

> *silver are corroded, and their corrosion will be a witness against you and will eat your flesh like fire. You have heaped up treasure in the last days.* (vs. 1-3)

In the New Testament, condemnations of wealthy people are usually attributed to a misuse of wealth. The first indictment of the rich has to do with the worthlessness of the worldly goods that they have so carefully assembled. James singles out four classes of material goods: riches, garments, gold, and silver. *Riches* are sometimes understood as a reference to crops. *Garments, gold,* and *silver* were the other most common forms of wealth in the ancient world. However, it is more likely that all these terms are used as a general terms for any wealth and reflect the traditional Old Testament and Jewish teaching about the foolishness of placing reliance upon perishable material goods. Crops rot, and fine clothes may be chewed up by moths. Gold and silver do not rust, they do become corroded. Gold can darken and silver tarnishes. Wealth brings no long-lasting benefit—its decay will testify against the rich at the day of judgement and bring a guilty verdict upon them. The reason for this judgment may simply be that the rich have concentrated on the accumulation of earthly treasure to the exclusion of heavenly treasure.

Jesus also warned about the fleeting accumulation of 'earthly treasures'. He said, *"Do not lay up for yourselves treasures on earth, where moth and rust destroy and where thieves break in and steal; "but lay up for yourselves treasures in heaven, where neither moth nor rust destroys and where thieves do not break in and steal. "For where your treasure is, there your heart will be also."* (Matthew 6:19-21).

Those who were enthusiastically accumulating wealth in James day were particularly sinful and especially foolish. They ignored the many signs of the rapidly approaching judgement.

God gives us our worldly possessions that we may honor him and do good with them; but if, instead of this, we sometimes sinfully hoard them up, we distrust the providence of God to bless us in the future as we give today. Scripture warns that wealth can be a particularly strong obstacle to Christian discipleship. *"Then Jesus said to His disciples,*

"Assuredly, I say to you that it is hard for a rich man to enter the kingdom of heaven" (Matt 19:23). He says it is hard, not impossible.

The miseries that are coming upon the rich refer not to earthly, temporal suffering, but to the condemnation and punishment that God will measure out to them on the day of judgement. When we come to the end of life, the question will be, "How much have you given?" not "How much have you gotten?"

THE DESIRE FOR WEALTH OFTEN LEADS TO GREEDINESS AND ABUSE.

> *"Indeed the wages of the laborers who mowed your fields, which you kept back by fraud, cry out; and the cries of the reapers have reached the ears of the Lord of Sabaoth. You have lived on the earth in pleasure and luxury; you have fattened your hearts as in a day of slaughter. You have condemned, you have murdered the just; he does not resist you."* (vs. 4-6)

A second charge that James levels against the rich is more specific; they have defrauded their workers of their pay. In a society where credit was not readily available, the failure to pay workers promptly could jeopardize life itself. They had no credit: VISA, MasterCard, or Discover. They lived largely, as many of us also do, day to day. They needed to stop by Safeway to buy bread, greens, and hamburger for the family to eat dinner that night. In those days, workers expected their pay at the end of the day. Indeed, this was commanded in the law: *"You shall not oppress a hired servant who is poor and needy, whether one of your brethren or one of the aliens who is in your land within your gates. "Each day you shall give him his wages, and not let the sun go down on it, for he is poor and has set his heart on it; lest he cry out against you to the Lord, and it be sin to you"* (Deuteronomy 24:14-15).

"You shall not cheat your neighbor, nor rob him. The wages of him who is hired shall not remain with you all night until morning" (Leviticus 19:13).

God is not deaf to the cries of injustice that rise both from wages withheld in fraud and from the laborers who have been oppressed by the rich. James declares, *"The cries of the reapers have reached the ears of the Lord of Sabaoth." Sabaoth* translates *host*, which is itself the adaptation of a Hebrew word that means *army*. The title *Lord of Sabaoth* (Lord of Hosts) thus pictures God as the almighty, powerful leader of a great army. James is convinced that the rich will not get away with their sin. Like Abel's blood 'cried out' as a witness having been murdered by his brother Cain, God is made aware of the sin and the pleading of the poor for vindication.

There has always been—and probably always will be—tension between the "haves and have-nots," between the "haves" and the "have not paid" for what they have, management and labor. We may be sure that whenever persons prosper at the expense and detriment of others God is displeased. The Lord may be temporarily silent about such injustice, but he hears the cries of those who are being oppressed.

James condemned rich people who acquired their wealth by exploiting other people. These wealthy employers withheld the wages of their workers. Either they did not pay them at all, or more likely, they paid them at sub-standard rates. Conditions like these are not nearly as common today as they were before labor unions turned the tables and assured most workers of their rights (sometimes with unfairness to employers!). However, there are still many workers, even in the United States, who are grossly underpaid. The migrant workers who follow the crops, for example, are not covered by minimum wage laws, have no "fringe-benefits," live in fearfully dirty housing, and must bring up their children with few educational or other advantages. Wal-Mart and other large chains have been accused of exploitation of third world workers.

The pursuit of a luxurious lifestyle that is selfish and unconcerned about other's needs is the third accusation brought against the rich. To be sure, James says simply that the rich *have lived on the earth in pleasure and luxury; you have fattened your hearts as in a day of slaughter.*

The rich are selfishly and ignorantly going about accumulating wealth for themselves and wastefully spending it on their own pleasures in the very day when God's judgment is imminently threatened. God's judgment could break in at any time—yet the rich, instead of acting to avoid that judgement, are, by their selfish indulgence, incurring greater guilt. They are like cattle being fattened for the kill.

The final accusation against the rich is that they have condemned and killed *the just. Condemn* is a judicial term, and suggests that the rich are using, and perhaps perverting, the legal processes available to them to accumulate property and to gain wealth. In the scramble for more wealth, the rich used their influence in courts of justice, and in the process were guilty of bringing condemnation and even death to innocent person who offered no resistance. What began as an interest in money ended as insensitivity to murder.

James does not condemn these people for being wealthy. He condemned them for the way they had acquired their money and for what they were doing with it. He condemned them of their greediness and abuse. Wealth honestly come by and wisely used is a blessing to its owners and to those it helps. Nevertheless, the rich people to whom James wrote left much to be desired in how they got their fortunes and in what they did with them.

THE MESSAGE FOR US.

Henry Jacobsen, *The Good life,* writes that every so often we read about some supposed "derelict" who dies in a shack in some city. When the person's corpse, dressed in dirty rags, is found, and his rat-infested shanty is torn down, workers discover thousands of dollars tucked away in the poor person's lumpy mattress. Instead of using the money to make themselves and other people comfortable, it was stashed it away where it helped neither them nor anyone else.

When a person hoards their money, they do not possess it—it possesses them. The Christian writer A. W. Tozer wrote, "Never possess anything. Have it, and use it, but never lay claim to it as yours." All that we have belongs to the Kingdom of God. We drive kingdom cars. Live in kingdom houses. Wear kingdom clothes and eat kingdom food. It all belongs to God.

Money is to be used. Christians are to be thoughtful about, considerate, and to prepare for the unseen realities of the future, but James seems to condemn storing up money while people suffer for lack of what it could do for them.

James was writing to people who had more than they needed of this world's goods. Few of us might admit that we have more than they need, but actually, it is true. If we were asked to bring in our extra clothes, clothes that no longer fit, or that we no longer like, or that are out of style; there would be an overabundance of clothes of every type and size. Shoes … pots and pans . . . outdated food in our cupboards . . .

The writer of Ecclesiastes in 10:18 (NIV) makes an interesting statement. There he says, *"If a man is lazy, the rafters sag; if his hands are idle, the house leaks. A feast is made for laughter, and wine makes life merry,* ***but money is the answer for everything.****"*

Contrary to what he says, and what many of us believe, ***money is not the answer for everything.*** Money brings joy temporarily; wealth if not used properly eventually results in misery. Though *wine can make us merry,* it will not be a house for us, nor a bed, nor clothing, nor provisions and portions for children; *but money,* if men have enough of it, will be all these. However, money is just a tool, of itself, it answers nothing; it will neither feed nor clothe; it is just the instrument of buying and selling, it answers all the physical needs of this present life. What is to be had of this world's goods may be had for money. However, money is not the answer for the things that trouble the soul; it will not procure the pardon of sin, the favor of God, the peace of conscience; it will not revive the soul, it cannot redeem those who are lost. It cannot buy un-prescripted sleep, genuine friends, or the love of another.

First Timothy 6:9 tells us that money can lead us astray, away from God. The apostle Paul writes, *"But those who desire to be rich fall into temptation and a snare, and into many foolish and harmful lusts which drown men in destruction and perdition. For the love of money is a root of all kinds of evil, for which some have strayed from the faith in their greediness, and pierced themselves through with many sorrows."*

It is not said, those that are rich, but those *who desire to be rich*, that is, that place their happiness in worldly wealth, that covet it excessively, that allow it to become a consuming ambition, and are eager and violent in the pursuit of it will suffer condemnation. Those that are such *fall into temptation and a snare, and* into *many foolish and hurtful lusts.*

****

Many have lots of money but are spiritually poor; they are poor in spirit. Some who think they are rich are living in poverty. They have much but are not fulfilled—some of us:

- Are relationship poor-have many acquaintances and don't know any of them well
- Have so many clothes, we "haven't a thing to wear"
- Eat so well we have to think about going on a diet
- Have every pill imaginable to cure our body's ills, because we "cannot afford to be sick"
- Have children that are loaded down with toys at birthdays and Christmas, and are being bored silly because there's nothing to do
- Have three degrees and feeling unfulfilled in our job
- Have two cars, a television in every room, a dishwasher, and then go "roughing it" by going camping to "get away from it all"
- Spend money on make-up, deodorants, colognes and designer clothes, and still being worried about the image we are projecting

People of every color living in America are healthy, middle-class, and yet still unhappy. Poverty is as much a matter of the soul, as it is the body. Many people think of wealth as the first step towards the good life. Money can buy things and make circumstances pleasant, but it is not true that money can buy fulfillment and lasting happiness.

In order to use money properly, little, or much, wisely, you must consider God. God is not nearly so much concerned with what you would do with a million dollars that you do not have as he is with how you use the ten dollars in your pocket. If you are to find real joy in what you have, you must recognize that you are a steward of what you have, and that your time and money really belong to God. As you obey him in using them, you will make better lives possible for others and, in so doing, will enjoy God's good life more richly yourself.

True wealth is made up only of things that we can carry into eternity. Each of us will have to give account to God for what he has placed in our hands. You may have . . ., but unless you know God, unless you know His Son as Lord and Savior, you will never know what real fulfillment is like and may find yourself like those on Oprah's show, rich but miserable.

What James is saying in chapter 5:1-6 is that if you have to choose between investing your money in the Kingdom of God or building a bigger bank account, invest in the things that will last forever. James tells business owners that if you have to choose between increasing your company's assets and giving your employees a fair wage, take care of your employees. He says that rather than investing your wealth in luxuries that will break down and increase your frustration, invest your wealth in the things that will truly give you peace and security for eternity.

REFLECTIONS AND MEDITATIONS

1. What are your feelings towards those who are wealthy?
2. How concerned are you about those who are less fortunate than you are?
3. Can you name a need or desire in our life money cannot satisfy?

CHAPTER 12

"PATIENCE AND THE LORD'S RETURN"

James 5:7-12

Christians ought to be patient and endure suffering.

"Therefore be patient, brethren, until the coming of the Lord." (James 5:7)

A young man, a Christian, went to an older believer to ask for prayer. "Will you please pray that I may be more patient?" he asked. The aged saint agreed. They knelt together and the man began to pray, "Lord, send this young man tribulation in the morning; send this young man tribulation in the afternoon; send this young man...." At that point, the young Christian blurted out, "No, no, I didn't ask you to pray for tribulation. I wanted you to pray for patience." "Ah," responded the wise Christian, "it's through tribulation that we learn patience."[13]

How many of us have a problem with a lack of patience. How many of us are willing to pay the price that is required in order to

---

13 http://www.sermoncentral.com/illustrations/sermon-illustration-phil-mellar-stories-godinthehardships-peace-9349.asp

gain patience? Most of us when we recognize the need for patience, we pray a prayer that goes something like this: "Lord, give me patience, and give it to me NOW!" However, patience, like most Christian characteristics, is one of those character traits that grows over time rather than being given to us overnight.

In this passage, James provides encouragement to Christians who have been oppressed by the rich to be patient and endure suffering. They are encouraged to hold-on, to be patient, and endure these hardships recognizing that they will ultimately be redeemed. James lets them and us know that there is a season to everything. There will come a season for the rich, for those who live mockingly of God, when the poor will be vindicated.

Those who are rich may not have oppressed us but we often find ourselves in situations where we also need to exert patience and perseverance. What are you in need of patience about today? I suspect today that some couple is in need of patience and perseverance in a marriage that is in the initial challenges of learning to live together. Others are challenged by a marriage that is seemingly going sour. Someone is in a career that for them lacks excitement and fulfillment and seems to be a dead end. Someone has a hope for a companion that is yet unfilled. Someone needs patience and perseverance in some circumstance. James challenges us with some things to do that we may endure the present and have a hope for the future.

WE ARE TO FORTIFY OURSELVES IN OUR FAITH.

> *"Therefore be patient, brethren, until the coming of the Lord. See how the farmer waits for the precious fruit of the earth, waiting patiently for it until it receives the early and latter rain. You also be patient. Establish your hearts, for the coming of the lord is at hand."* (vs. 7, 8)

A famous Christian lecturer was speaking of the desirable characteristics to be found and cultivated in the Christian teacher.

He suggested that, especially for teachers of the young, ten traits were to be considered. "Number one," he states, "is patience. Without it, the teacher cannot survive the rigors of preparation and presentation. Number two, is a Christian commitment to his goal. Without this, he will not achieve the best results. Number three," he added, "is patience. Number four, is a proper respect for and knowledge of the Word of God. Number five is patience." By that time, the audience got his point. Patience in teaching, in witnessing, in all aspects of Christian life, will accomplish what nothing else can. [14]

Patience is clearly the key idea in this passage. James says, *be patient.* James urges his brethren, that is, Christians, to be patient in the face of mistreatment at the hands of the rich. The word *patient* in the Greek is a compound word composed of two words "long" and "temper", or long-tempered, the opposite of "short-tempered" that we know all too well.

Specifically, James encourages patience unto *the coming of the Lord.* To demonstrate an example of patience James points to the farmer who has learned patience by long experience. The farmer knows that he cannot plant his grain until the early rains, coming in late October or early November, have softened the soil so that it can be plowed to receive the seed. He also knows that there is little he can do except wait for the latter rains, the rains of winter and early spring to bring the crop to fruition.

From this reference to the common practice of farmers, we can conclude several important lessons. First, there is a certain order of events in the course of nature, and worrying and fretting will not hasten or change this order. Some things are related to time and just require us to hang in there. Some of us have committed ourselves to financial obligations; rather than trying to hit the lotto, or becoming involved in some illegal endeavor trying to get out of debt, we diligently need to continue to pay the monthly payment.

---

[14] *Standard Lesson Commentary*, (Cincinnati, OH: Standard Publishing, 1983-1984), 331

Incidentally, marriage is not like your car payment. You do not signup up for 36, or 48 months, or 60 months and count down until it is paid off. It is a lifetime commitment and changes often occur slowly over time.

In the second place, we have certain responsibilities. The farmer must wait for God to send the rain. However, he must be prepared to plow and plant when the rains do come. In the midst of whatever you are going through you must not become complacent but prepare yourself for the future. If you are a single in search of a mate, do not just waste your time waiting. Work on making yourself more desirable physically, more desirable intellectually, financially, and spiritually. There is work to be done in anticipation of what God may bring your way, or if you are one that God has called to be single, you may be wasting precious time.

Finally, we should learn from this reference that there is only so much we can do. The farmer has to depend upon God for the rain the soil and the sunshine needed to produce the crop. The apostle Paul declared of those in Corinth who had come to believe in Christ, *"I planted, Apollos watered, but God gave the increase"* (1 Cor 3:6). We have a part to play in our success, whether in our marriage, in our career, in our sharing of our faith, whatever. We must plant and water seeds for success but always recognize and depend upon God for the *increase.*

How long are we to be patient? Many a married couple on the throws of divorce has asked this question. How long do I have to put up with this, how long am I to be patient? Life is too short! James would say to be patient "*Until the coming of the Lord.*" However, when might that be? Who knows—could be today, tomorrow, or years into the future.

The early Christian conviction that the *second coming* of Jesus was near, or imminent, meant that they fully believed that it could transpire within a short period—not that it had to. They, like Jesus, knew neither the day nor the hour (Mark 13:32); but they acted, and taught others to act, as if their generation could be the last. Almost twenty centuries later, we live in exactly the same situation; our own decade could be the last in human history. We must therefore, act and live as if our generation could be the last. James' advice to us, no matter what circumstance we may be in, it is the same as it was to his first-century, *"Be patient. Establish your hearts, for the coming of the lord is at hand."* (vs. 8)

What we all need, no matter what we are going through, is to *establish* our hearts. What does that mean? It means that we need to firm up our faith in the midst of temptations and trials. As we wait patiently for our Lord Jesus to return, we need to fortify ourselves for the struggle against sin and with difficult circumstances. Someone has said, "The secret of patience is doing something else in the meantime." James says in the meantime that we are to establish ourselves in our faith. Build up our hearts; fortify our faith.

A CONDEMNATION TO AVOID.

> *"Do not grumble against one another, brethren, lest you be condemned. Behold, the Judge is standing at the door!"* (vs. 9)

A typical American family was driving home from church one Sunday. Dad was fussing about the sermon being too long and sort of boring. Mom said she thought the organist played too loudly during the second hymn they sang. Sis, who was a music major in college, said she thought the soloist sang about a half note off key during most of her song. Grandma said she could not hear very well -- since they were sitting toward the back. As they pulled in the driveway, little Willie, who had listened to all of this, started to fuss about the woman who sat in front of him with that big hat. Then he paused, nudged his dad, and said, "But, Dad, you gotta admit, it was a pretty good show for a nickel." Ouch! [15]

To many people, attending church is a lot like watching a show. The better the entertainment, the more they enjoy coming.

---

[15] Charles R. Swindoll, *The Tale of the Tardy Oxcart and 1,501 Other Stories*, (Nashville, TN: Thomas Nelson, 1998)

However, the less they like what they see and hear, the more they grumble and complain. Let the "show" get very bad, and there is no way most people are going to sit through it. Yet, we have to admit that the "price of admission" is still pretty hard to beat. Compared to what the public is willing to pay for live theater or a professional ball game, it is still "a pretty good show for a nickel." Or maybe a quarter, dollar . . .

Some people seem to have sour dispositions and create all kinds of problems by their complaining. Other persons become complainers when circumstances go wrong. James is not talking here about people who have genuine problems but about people whose motive is to create division. Some have things to be concerned about.

The story is told of a man whose wife had just bought a new line of expensive cosmetics absolutely guaranteed to make her look years younger. She sat in front of the mirror for what had to be hours applying the "miracle" products. Finally, when she was done, she turned to her husband and said, "Hon, honestly now, what age would you say I am?" He nodded his head in assessment, and carefully said, "Well, hon, judging from your skin, twenty. Your hair, mmmm, eighteen. Your figure, twenty-five." "Oh, you're so sweet!" Her husband interrupted, "Well, hang on, I'm not done adding it up yet." That might make a wife swear or say something she should not. As we all know, there are many things that happen in life that could make us grumble, gripe, complain, and perhaps even cuss.

In any kind of relationship, continued grumbling and complaining against another can only disrupt the fellowship. James reminds his readers that such behavior invites judgment from the Lord. Indeed, he says, the judge, the Lord Jesus, stands at the door ready to bring judgment. Would Jesus find us grumbling at one another if he came to the door of our house today, if he walked into our church? Our criticism of one another places us in danger of judgment. This warning is similar to, and may be influenced by, Jesus' well-known prohibition: *'Judge not, that you be not judged'* (Matthew 7:1).

The coming Lord is judge of the unbeliever and the judge of the Christian. The nearness of the last days, or Christ coming, is a warning to examine our behavior so that when the one whose footsteps are nearing finally knocks at the door, we may be prepared to open. One person said, "Rather than fearing what is to come, we are to be faithful till Christ returns. Instead of fearing the dark, we're to be lights as we watch and wait."

As children in a school classroom look out for their teacher's soon return, God's children should be on guard for Christ's return. In doing so, good behavior and mutual harmony are essential. Do not grumble because you do not have what you want--be thankful you do not get what you deserve. Some of us deserved to be flogged, left out in the cold, to go hungry and homeless—to experience the wrath of God.

A WONDERFUL EXAMPLE TO FOLLOW.

> *"My brethren, take the prophets, who spoke in the name of the Lord, as an example of suffering and patience. Indeed we count them blessed who endure. You have heard of the perseverance of Job and seen the end intended by the Lord--that the Lord is very compassionate and merciful."* (vs. 10-11)

"Where have you been, Father?" asked the son of Abraham Lincoln. "To the war department," he answered. "Any news?" "Yes, plenty of news, but no good news. It is dark, dark everywhere." He then reached forth one of his long arms and took a small Bible from a stand near the head of the sofa, opened its pages, and was soon absorbed in reading. Fifteen minutes passed, and on glancing at the sofa his wife observed that the face of the president was more cheerful. His dejected expression was gone, and his countenance was lighted up with new resolution and hope. Wondering at the marked change, and desiring to know what book of the Bible had comforted Mr. Lincoln, she walked gently around the sofa and saw that he was reading the comforting book of Job. In spite of the tribulation of Job, Lincoln was comforted in the hope that God oversaw his entire situation from beginning to end.

James says the prophets are an example of suffering and patience. God's messengers, in every age, have traveled a hard road. If you think being a Christian is hard, become a prophet or preacher. The fact that they *spoke in the name of the Lord* is added to make it clear that the suffering endured by them was a result not of wrongdoing, but specifically of their faithful adherence to the will of God.

Indeed we count them blessed who endure. Those who faithfully endured are called *blessed.* To be blessed is not, of course, the same as being happy. Happiness is tied to happenings. If the right thing is happening then you are happy. *Blessings* on the other hand are the result of the approval and reward of God. The prophets received reward, because they were faithful in tribulation.

You have heard of the perseverance of Job. Interestingly, James did not say the prophet Job had "patience," but that he had "*perseverance.*" Job endured and he was steadfast, though he was impatient with God! Job submission was not without question. He struggled and questioned, and sometimes even defied, but the flame of faith was never extinguished in his heart. He never abandoned his faith; in the midst of his incomprehension, he clung to God and continued to hope in him (Job 1:21; 2:10; 16:19-21; 19:25-27).

It makes good sense to take the phrase *and seen the end intended by the Lord* as a reference to the end or outcome of Job's situation, which the Lord eventually brought about; the restoration of his family and fortune (Job 42:13). The Lord honored Job's perseverance with multiplied blessings (Job 42:12). Certainly, James does not mean that patience in suffering will always be rewarded by material prosperity; too many examples, in the Old Testament and the New Testament, prove this wrong. However, he does seek to encourage our faithful, patient endurance of affliction by reminding us of the blessing that we receive for such faithfulness from our merciful and compassionate God.

Hundreds of eyes were fixed on the quarter miler as he broke from the starting blocks in quest of a state high school record. As the race progressed, he ran with a deceptive ease, a long stride, and an obvious objective, moving farther ahead of the field. When he broke the tape, he owned the record easily.

While the photographers and reporters gathered around him immediately, and while the runner was receiving the congratulations of other runners, most of the spectators never saw another fellow, still running toward the finish line. All the other competitors had ended the course some time before he half ran, half fell, across the line—dead last, but he finished!

Perseverance is the name of the game, whether we speak of running an athletic race or the Christian life. Good beginnings help, but it is finishing that counts.

****

When Mike Kollin was a linebacker for the Dolphins and a graduate of Auburn University, his former college coach, Shug Jordan, asked him if he would do some recruiting for him. Mike said, "Sure, coach. What kind of player are you looking for?" The coach said, "Well, Mike, you know there's that fellow, you knock him down, he just stays down?" Mike said, "We don't want him, do we, coach?" "No, that's right. Then there's that fellow, you knock him down and he gets up, but you knock him down again and he stays down." Mike answered, "We don't want him either, do we, coach?" Coach said, "No, but Mike, there's a fellow, you knock him down, he gets up. Knock him down, he gets up. Knock him down, he gets up. Knock him down, he gets up." Mike said, "That's the guy we want, isn't it, coach?" The coach answered, "No, we don't want him either. I want you to find that guy who's knocking everybody down. That's the guy we want!" [16]

Most of us are on the receiving versus the giving end of life's knockdowns. When you are knocked down, when you get

---

16 http://www.sermoncentral.com/Illustration/Opening Joke: Coach Shug Jordan At Auburn, Text Illustration shared by Chris Jordan, Beausejour Community Church

discouraged, when your marriage is not working, and your job is not either. When you have buried yourself in a mountain of debt and something happens to add another bill, when you keep getting knocked down, keep getting up. Life will continue to try to knock you down, but keep getting up. The coach may want the one doing the knocking down, but God wants and encourages the one who will keep getting up.

James says of the poor, those who have been knocked down by the rich that they are to wait and be watchful, the Lord is on His way. The rich may be having their day now but Christians are encouraged to be patient for our season is coming. While waiting we are not to be engaged in divisiveness towards each other but to maintain a spirit of unity.

There is more to life than this life and God will set all things straight, He will correct all errors; He will make everything right in the next life. We may suffer for a season but there is a greater, better, and longer season coming! *You also be patient. Establish your hearts, for the coming of the lord is at hand"* (vs. 8).

The song says,
We fall down but we get up (3x)
"For a saint is a sinner who fell down and got up."[17]

If you have fallen down, been knocked down, tripped and stumbled, and tumbled down—get up! Christ gave his life that we might get up from sin. You do not have to stay down. God is inviting you today to get up!

REFLECTIONS AND MEDITATIONS

1. Are you living life in anticipation of God answering your prayer?

---

[17] Donnie McClurkin, Writer Kyle David Matthews, Copyright: Universal Music, Brentwood Benson Publishers

2. When things are not as you think they should be, are you inclined to grumble or to deal with it in a more positive manner?
3. When confronted with trials and tribulations, is your focus on the disaster or are you anticipating God's deliverance?

CHAPTER 13

"THE POWER OF PRAYER"

James 5:13-20

The power of prayer is clearly manifested by those ordained elders in conjunction with the power of God to bring forth physical and spiritual healing, and in the cleansing of one's heart and prayer relationships for each other.

And the prayer of faith will save the sick, and the Lord will raise him up. And if he has committed sins, he will be forgiven. (James 5:15)

Knowing how to pray, knowing what to do, on behalf of those who are sick is often quite the challenge. However, whether it is a physical illness, a psychosomatic/emotional disorder, or some spiritual anomaly, we are called to pray. The following is a prayer by Norwegian theologian Ole Hallesby that acknowledges the ability of God to heal but also his sovereign will:

"Lord, if it will be to Your glory, heal suddenly. If it will glorify You more, heal gradually; if it will glorify You even more, may your servant remain

> sick awhile; and if it will glorify Your name still more, take him to Yourself in heaven." [18]

There are those who say that God's will is for us never to be sick and that if we have enough faith we can be healed of every disease. The reality of death, through which we all must pass, seems to invalidate that argument. I have officiated at the funerals of too many great saints of God to believe that to be true. To my knowledge all the disciples, apostles, and great saints of old are dead. All of us will die from something: disease, accident, or old age. Hebrews 9:27 declares *"And as it is appointed for men to die once."* Yet in spite of those facts, we are called to pray in the face of the seemingly inevitable.

No matter what the affliction, the greatest assistance any believer can offer another is faithful prayer. Prayer is clear evidence of care. Prayer is the "hotline" to the One who can provide for any need no matter how complex or impossible it may seem.

James 5:14-16 is the only passage in the New Testament epistles that directly addresses the question of physical healing. One finds three actions in the healing ritual: prayer, anointing, and the calling out of the name of Jesus. Prayer is clearly the topic of this section, being mentioned in every verse. James wants us to understand something here, as it relates healing, about ourselves and about this matter of prayer. Let us see what he has to say.

OUR ENTIRE LIFE IS TO BE CENTERED IN GOD.

> *Is anyone among you suffering? Let him pray. Is anyone cheerful? Let him sing psalms.* (vs. 13)

This verse implies that our entire life is to be centered in God. When we are discouraged, we are to ask his help. When we feel cheerful, we are to thank him for his goodness. This amounts to

---

18 Parsons Technology, Bible Illustrator, Topic: Healing, Index: 1538-1541, Date: 8/1989.1

keeping in touch with him at all times. Prayer and praise are to be the overall attitudes of our personal Christian life.

However, the two greatest weaknesses in the average church today are the areas of prayer and praise. The reason for these weaknesses may be traced to our spiritual insensitivity, self-reliance, and self-sufficiency. In spite of all or our seeming resources, there is much need for prayer and much cause to praise.

For those who were suffering difficult times, because of their faith, from illness, poverty, or possibly from business loss, James' solution was not to grumble or engage in an extended pity party. Instead, he suggested that they pray. Such a prayer might be that the cause of suffering be removed, or it might be that one would bear the suffering with strength and grace. Suffering should call us to a time of prayer.

However, serving the Lord is not always a painful experience. Sometimes it brings joy. Such happy occasions should lead to singing; either as a part of congregational worship or in personal songs as one goes about his or her work. The joy of God's sufficiency ought to inspire us to praise God for his goodness.

Yes, our suffering should elicit prayer, and our sufficiency should elicit praise. James challenges believers to pray or praise in whatever situation we may find ourselves. He calls us to center our lives in God. If our life is centered in self, it will ultimately lead to misery: but if it is centered in God, it will ultimately lead to peace.

A REMEDY FOR WHAT AILS US.

> *Is anyone among you sick? Let him call for the elders of the church, and let them pray over him, anointing him with oil in the name of the Lord. And the prayer of faith will save the sick, and the Lord will raise him up. And if he has committed sins, he will be forgiven.* (vs. 14, 15)

A great deal of misunderstanding has resulted from these verses. The heart of the problem lies in just what James meant when he referred to the "*sick.*"

Who are the sick?

Actually, there is no reason to consider "*sick*" as referring exclusively to physical illness. Some theologians believe that James was not referring to the bedridden, the diseased, or the ill. Instead, they believe he wrote to those who had grown weary, who had become weak both morally and spiritually in the midst of suffering. These ones should call for the help of the elders of the church. The early church leaders were instructed (1 Thessalonians 5:14, NIV) to *"encourage the timid"* and *"help the weak."*[19]

This being true, James says that the elders should pray over him and anoint him with oil. James point is that the weak and weary would be refreshed, encouraged, and uplifted by the elders who rubbed oil on the persons' heads and prayed for them. The elders' prayer offered in faith will make the sick person, that is the "weary one," well (i.e., restore him from discouragement and spiritual defeat), and *the Lord will raise him up.* [20]

Others believe it is best to view James anointing as a physical action with symbolic significance. Since the symbolism of 'anointing' (Old Testament anointing of the tabernacle utensils, priest's robes, etc.) is usually associated with the setting apart or consecrating of someone or something for God, we are probably to understand this as the symbolism intended in the action. As the elders pray for the sick person, they also set that person apart for "God's special attention."

An appeal to the elders to pray for those downtrodden and weak in faith would be entirely appropriate. While this is true, it impossible to eliminate the consideration of the symbolic dimension. In reality, it is probably both an encouragement to those who are weak and weary symbolically setting them apart and consecrating them for "God's special attention and care."

---

[19] The Bible Knowledge Commentary, NT, 834

[20] Moo, 180

Who are the Elders?

Not every elder was necessarily an old man; and conversely, an old man was not necessarily an elder. Elders were those spiritual leaders who were recognized for their maturity in the faith, who acted in the name of God and by the authority of God. It was an office that no man could take upon himself but to which he must be duly chosen by those who were already elders and to which, after his choice, he was ordained by the laying on of their hands. Therefore, it is natural that they, with their deep and rich experience, should be called on to pray for healing. They, above all, should be able to discern the will of the Lord and to pray with the faith that recognizes and receives God's gift of healing.

We have here something unique in James; a concrete reference to the official organization of the Christian community under the rule of elders who had been formally ordained to their office. Those ordained in our church are ministers and deacons. The oil, when applied by the *duly authorized* elders of the church, in conjunction with their prayer, would have a particular effectiveness.

The effectiveness of the prayers of the elders presupposes their spiritual connection with God. It presupposes that they are men and women of God who are living right and holy and who are able to make a prayer connection on behalf of those who are sick. There is a message in here for those of us who are ministers and deacons that in order to be effective and to accomplish what James assigns us with, we must be spiritual. If our lives are not as they should be when called upon to pray for the sick we can no more affect the process of healing than someone who is an unbeliever. I wonder sometimes if the reason people are not satisfied with the elders praying is that they do not see them living out their lives and position faithfully.

Sometimes elders and ministers are criticized because they do not always carry out this ministry, but they may fail because they are not aware of all the illnesses in the congregation. The ill person has a responsibility to inform the leaders of his or her need. Anyone who has experienced an illness knows how encouraging and helpful visits and prayer can be.

The Use of Oil

The practice of anointing with oil is mentioned only one other time in the New Testament. Mark 6:13 declares, *"And they cast out many demons, and anointed with oil many who were sick, and healed them."* Unfortunately, no more explanation of the practice is given there than here in James.

In general, there are two main possibilities for the anointing. First, it may have a practical purpose. Oil was widely used in the ancient world as a medicine. Persons who have been ill often find that their skin is dry and parched. An application of oil would have a softening, soothing effect. The other possibility may be that anointing with oil had a religious purpose. As the elders prayed, they would anoint the sick person to symbolize that that person was being set apart for God's special attention and care. [21] This second possibility would seem to be the best choice.

The Prayer of Faith

The power of faith opens the gates to God's power. We must understand that the promise of healing is not unrestricted. Healing will follow a prayer of faith only if that healing is within the will of God. All of us probably know of cases where healing occurred contrary to all medical prognosis. However, we also know many more cases where death or continued illness followed numerous and fervent prayers. Our responsibility in such times is to pray in faith and truth allowing the outcome to be God's will.

The faith is that of the one who prays, that is, the elders who have *sanctioned* healing power, not that of the sick person (who may or may not be in a condition to exercise much of anything). That

---

[21] Moo, 178

this power is God's power comes in the parallel statement "*the Lord will raise him up.*"

Every prayer that we utter must come within the framework of God's will. Jesus in his ministry did not heal every sick person in Palestine. Apparently, it was not God's will that all be healed. Even though we do not understand this, we are to pray believing for healing until we see otherwise. Our responsibility is to pray, God's responsibility is to heal. If he chooses not to do so, then he is responsible for that. Absence of healing is never due to lack of ability on God's part.

The Forgiveness of Sin

Like the healing, the forgiveness of sin is conditional. Forgiveness requires sincere repentance on the part of the sinner. Many physically ill Christians have called on elders to pray for them and to anoint them with oil, but a sizable percentage of them have remained sick. For many the greatest healing they need may not be physical but spiritual, James would seem to allude to this in saying, *if he has sinned, he will be forgiven.*

SICKNESS AND SIN ARE CLOSELY RELATED.

> *Confess your trespasses to one another, and pray for one another, that you may be healed. The effective, fervent prayer of a righteous man avails much.* (vs. 16)

In Jewish thought sin, sickness, and confession were closely associated, and James' Jewish Christian readers would have readily understood this. Certainly not all sickness results from sin, yet much of it does. The confession of sins both to God and to the offended can remove barriers that allow healing to enter. Many problems transpire in our lives, in our family, and in our church from strife and unforgiveness.

We know from Jesus' words in John 9:3 that physical disability is not always a result of sin. Doctors today tell us that a large percentage of illness is psychosomatic--that is, it results from people's inability to cope with the pressures of modern life. However, guilt feelings can cause illness, and James suggests that there may at times be a relationship between illness and past sins. God, however, stands ready to forgive a sick person.

We do not believe that every illness is God's punishment for sin, but that much suffering does result from sinful habits, and a guilty conscience from concealed sin will inhibit healing. Much suffering does come as a direct result of a sinful life-style, yet, we must recognize that the innocent often have to suffer through no fault of their own. We know that many illnesses are due in part to the wrong kinds of mental attitudes. When one has cleansed one's soul by the confession of sins, that person's body is given a better chance to regain its strength.

James may have had in view the confession of the sick person to the elder who came to pray. Such confession would enable the elder better to counsel the penitent. However, let us not be so overtaken with the command to confess our sins that we overlook the equally important command to pray for one another. The subject of this whole passage is prayer, not confession.

The effective, fervent prayer of a righteous man avails much. The word here translated prayer is different from that used in the first part of this verse and verse 15. Whereas the word used earlier encompasses all forms of prayer, the word here means "petition" or "begging." The word translated in the King James Version as *effectual fervent* is the root of our word energetic. Thus, we may say regarding prayer, "The energetic begging of a righteous man is very powerful" *(Standard Lesson Commentary, 1983-1984, 333).* Here again, we come face to face with the requirement of those who intercede. They must be righteous for their prayer to be effective. A believer who is living holy in close relationship with God—his or her prayer is dynamic. It works. It produces real, specific results. It does not change God's mind, but it is the means that he has ordained that his purposes should be fulfilled.

However, the power possessed by prayer is not limited to elders, to 'super saints'; the righteous man simply designates anyone who is whole-heartedly committed to God and sincerely seeking to do his will.

****

The story is told about a young pastor who goes to pray with an older woman. She's near death; she's in the hospital lying on the pillow, gasping for breath. He visits with her, and then he says, "I need to go, but would you like to have prayer before I go?" The old woman says, "Yes." He says, "Well, what would you like us to pray for today?" And she says, "I'd like to pray I'd be healed, of course." The young pastor gasps but goes on, "Lord, we pray for your sustaining presence with this sick sister. And if it be thy will, we pray that she will be restored to health and to service. But if it's not thy will, we certainly hope that she will adjust to her circumstances."

Suddenly the old woman opens her eyes and sits up in bed. She throws her feet over the side of the bed. She stands up. She says, "I think I'm healed!" And she runs out the door. The last the pastor sees, she's running down the hall toward the nurses' station, saying "Look! Look at me!" The pastor goes down the steps, goes out to the parking lot. Before he opens the door of his car, he looks up and says, "Don't you ever do that to me again!" [22]

To intercede on someone's behalf in prayer, we must have sensitivity to their needs, engage in diligent supplication for those needs, recognize the significance of those needs, and pray with a sense of expectancy. We have to expect that God is going to do something. We ought never just pray as a matter of fact. Whether we pray, anoint with oil, do both, we ought to have a sense of setting that person aside for God's special attention and care and expect that he is going to do something.

Although the elders are called to anoint the sick and pray, it does not exclude the congregation at large from the same task.

---

22 Parsons Technology, Bible Illustrator, Topic: Prayer, Subtopic: Power of, Index: 4193, Date: 6/1998.2154, Title: Humor: Unexpected Healing

James makes it clear that the church at large is to pray for healing. Therefore, while not denying that some in the church may have the gift of healing, James encourages all Christians, and especially those charged with pastoral oversight, to be active in prayer for healing. You do not have to wait for the pastor, ministers and deacons to come and pray. We can do that ourselves. God is our comforter when we face trouble in life and we must be quick to go to Him in prayer.

Are you in need of healing today? It all begins in a relationship with the One who can heal and make a difference in your life. Is any among you afflicted? The prayer of faith shall save the sick—the physically sick, the spiritually sick, the sin-sick and the afflicted—and *the Lord shall raise him up.*

REFLECTIONS AND MEDITATIONS

1. Are your prayers focused on problems of life or on the Provider of solutions?
2. The healing of sickness, either physically or spiritually is subject to the will of God—what part do you play?
3. How aware are you of the need to keep yourself spiritually in shape to be able to exercise prayerful help to others?

CHAPTER 14

"CONTROLLING THE ATMOSPHERE"

James 5:17-18

Through faith and prayer, we have the ability to control the atmosphere around us.

> *"Elijah was a man with a nature like ours, and he prayed earnestly that it would not rain; and it did not rain on the land for three years and six months. And he prayed again, and the heaven gave rain, and the earth produced its fruit." (James 5:17-18)*

First Kings 17:1 tells us of the prophet Elijah. He was a prophet of God during the reign of King Ahab, King of Israel. First Kings 16:33 tells us, *"Ahab did more to provoke the Lord God of Israel to anger than all the kings of Israel who were before him."* King Ahab did more to promote idolatry than all the kings before him. He took to wife *"Jezebel the daughter of Ethbaal, king of the Sidonians; and he went and served Baal and worshiped him. Then he set up an altar for Baal in the temple of Baal, which he had built in Samaria. And Ahab made a wooden image"* (16:31-33).

The Canaanites worshiped Baal as the sun god and as the storm god—he is usually depicted holding a lightning bolt—who defeated enemies and produced crops. They also worshiped him as a fertility god who provided children. Baal worship was rooted in sensuality and involved ritualistic prostitution in the temples. During the reign of Ahab and Jezebel, at the height of Baal worship in Israel, in the midst of the culture and climate of idolatry and great immorality comes a word to King Ahab from a prophet by the name of Elijah. It is not stated how Elijah's prophecy came to him, but we have record of what he told the king. *And Elijah the Tishbite, of the inhabitants of Gilead, said to Ahab, "As the Lord God of Israel lives, before whom I stand, there shall not be dew nor rain these years, except at my word"* (1 Kings 17:1). What a profound statement! What presumption! What audacity! What courage to stand in front of the king and proclaim a nation-wide drought. In the third year of the drought, Elijah again is called to confront the king.

First Kings 18:1-2 tells us, *"And it came to pass after many days that the word of the Lord came to Elijah, in the third year, saying, "Go, present yourself to Ahab, and I will send rain on the earth." So Elijah went to present himself to Ahab; and there was a severe famine in Samaria."* A great contest ensues on Mount Carmel, between Elijah and *the four hundred and fifty prophets of Baal, and the four hundred prophets of Asherah, who eat at Jezebel's table"* to determine who the real God of Israel is. The contest results in the death of all the prophets of Baal and Asherah; and the Lord God being affirmed as the real God of Israel. The evidence was overwhelming, and the people "fell prostrate and cried, 'The LORD–he is God! The LORD–he is God!'" (vs. 39). It then begins to rain. If you have not read 1 Kings 17 and 18, do so,

In our text, James, as we learned in the previous chapter, on the heels of admonishing those who are sick: weak, weary, and physically ill to call for the elders of the church to pray for them gives a historical example of the power of faith and prayer. It is a strong example, one that has supernatural circumstances, but is the result of an ordinary man.

As we view the example of Elijah, in light to the climate and culture of our land being one increasingly inclined towards immorality, death, and destruction; we need to ask ourselves what ability do we have to control the atmosphere, to adjust and regulate the spiritual thermostats of our country, community, church, and personal lives. Let us see if we can find any clues from the testimony of Elijah.

ELIJAH WAS A MAN.

"Elijah was a man with a nature like ours . . ." (vs. 17a)

James makes the point clear that Elijah was not a super-saint. *He was a man with a nature like ours*, with *like* passions as *ours*. Had he not inserted this statement we might be tempted to use the excuse that he operated with supernatural ability, outside of our ability to effect change.

If James had said that Peter was "a man just like us," we would not have much trouble with that because Peter was often saying the wrong thing, putting his mouth in gear before his brain was engaged. So if James had said, "Peter was a man just like us." we would say, "Yes, we can certainly see that." Or if James had said, "David was a man just like us," we could say, "We can see that, too." David writes in his Psalms of his frustrations, and searching for God's will, and of wondering who he can trust. David sinned. David had trouble with his kids. Indeed, David was a man just like us. However, James does not mention them. He says, "Elijah was a man just like us." In addition, the rest of the passage says that when Elijah prayed earnestly that it would not rain, God held back the rain. Then three and one-half years later Elijah prayed that it would rain, and the rains came. As a prophet from God, Elijah did some very extraordinary things. However, James' message is that Elijah was just an ordinary person, and that God can take ordinary people and accomplish extraordinary things.[23]

Elijah was just an ordinary man who was a servant of a most extraordinary God. He modeled the kind of faith in God that

---

23 http://www.sermoncentral.com/*sermons/Just Like Us, Melvin Newland*

James had spoken of in the previous verses. James 5:18 records, *"The effective, fervent prayer of a righteous man avails much.* Elijah was a man who understood the power of prayer. The earnest prayer of a righteous person has great power and wonderful results.[24]

PRAY WAS HIS VEHICLE FOR CHANGE.

> *"And he prayed earnestly that it would not rain; and it did not rain on the land for three years and six months"* (vs. 17b-c)

I have prayed for God to not let it snow on a particular Sunday. I have prayed when traveling for God to guide me through storms and rain. I have seen where the climatic elements lined up with my prayer. Some might consider it coincidence, but they were not the one who prayed. They were not the one with a sense of expectancy. I believe God answers prayer, even in the matter of controlling the environment. However, my prayers were private.

For someone to declare publically the rain to stop for years would require an awesome faith. It does not say if Elijah knew how long the rains would be withheld, but he knew it would be years. Do you have the audacity to believe that your prayer can control the atmosphere? The audacity to think that your prayer can control the natural elements? The audacity to declare in the face of officials, the king what would and would not be, to declare a universal drought across the land. The vision of drought was not his it was of God.

Because he prayed, we can attribute the supernatural act to God and not to Elijah. He was not the one who controlled the atmosphere; he only made a prayerful request. God is always the one who is ultimately in control. Miracles begin and end with God. In God's timing, Elijah *". . . prayed again, and the heaven gave rain, and the earth produced its fruit"* (vs. 18).

---

[24] http://www.sermoncentral.com/sermons/Experiencing the Power of Prayer, Stephan Brown

Prayer is not meant to inform God of things He does not know or is not willing to do. Prayer is meant for us, to remind us that we need Him.

- We need to pray if we want to see our children do well at school
- We need to pray if we want to see our problems solved
- We need to pray if we want to see success in our work
- We need to pray if we want to experience healing, health, and wholeness
- We need to pray if we want to experience forgiveness, cleansing, and holiness

God is sovereign and all-powerful. He can do what He wants, yet God works in response to our prayer. James 4:2 declares, *"You do not have, because you do not ask."*

CAN WE CHANGE THE ATMOSPHERE?

Can our prayers actually change things? Can God's will on earth be frustrated or not accomplished if we do not pray? Does God need us to pray or does He just want us to pray? The great theologian and evangelist John Wesley says, "God does nothing on the earth save in answer to believing prayer."

The climate, the atmosphere, in our country right now is one of death and destruction. We have recently experienced much tragedy:

- Boston Marathon
- West Texas fertilizer plant blowup
- Century 21 theatre
- Shooting at the Sandy Hook elementary school
- Earthquake in China

No matter whether we are considering extreme conditions such as these or those who are weary, weak, and physically sick the ministry we are called to provide is largely the same. As the people of God, we need to consider both comfort and a cure.

Put yourself in a pastoral situation for a moment ministering to someone injured in the Boston Marathon. What do you say to someone in the hospital who just a few days ago was healthy enough to run a 26 mile marathon and now finds themselves with missing limbs? What do you say to someone who has lost a loved one? What comfort do we provide?

First, we need to help them understand where the blame needs to be applied. The tendency when we, as believers, find ourselves at a loss is to question God. God! Why me, why now, why this? What have I done? Is this the reward for my faithfulness, my obedience? Is there some hidden sin in my life?

In spite of wanting somehow to place the blame on God, we need to recognize that incidents like these are the result of the free-will, which God affords each of us. We are not created robots. We are given the will to operate freely in this life to choose to do good, or choose to do evil. In the case of shootings and bombings, we see that someone chose evil. It is both the privilege and the curse on humanity to be able to choose and to be able to choose badly.

The devil is the source of sin and destruction. The Bible declares that the devil comes *"to steal, and to kill, and to destroy"* (John 10:10). He is the source of all that is evil and we can be assured that he controls the hearts of those inclined towards destruction.

Additionally, some things happen just because we are living in a fallen world. Accidental explosions happen often through no fault of our own, but because we live in an imperfect world and sometimes the world's imperfections accumulate and are manifested in disastrous ways.

We must be careful not to blame God, but recognize that we have a God who loves us through it all. In spite of life's difficulties, which are sometimes extreme such as in the loss of extremities and life, God is still able to make all things work together for our good. Romans 8:28 (KJV) declares, *"And we know that all things work together for good to them that love God, to them who are the called according to his purpose.*

Second, we must help them understand the cure. The other significant question people ask is what can we do about it? How can we prevent this from happening again? What can we do?

The response of law enforcement is more police officers, metal detectors, better surveillance, and more laws. Although those things provide for a good defense, they do little to deal with the issue of the sin. Sin, as manifested in immorality, idolatry, self-reliance, self-promotion, and self-satisfaction, is at the heart of destruction. It was the problem in Elijah's day. James said that the vehicle available to Elijah to confront the problem of evil in his day was prayer.

In 2 Chronicles 7:13 (KJV) God had given Solomon a future circumstance of the penalty of the nation of Israel falling into idolatry and then followed it with a cure, one not unlike Elijah experienced. God said, *"When I shut up heaven and there is no rain, or command the locusts to devour the land, or send pestilence among My people . . ."* There would be a penalty for the nation's immorality. In 2 Chronicles 7:14 (KJV) he gave them a cure, *"If my people, which are called by my name, shall humble themselves, and pray, and seek my face, and turn from their wicked ways; then will I hear from heaven, and will forgive their sin, and will heal their land."*

The cure then and the cure now is prayer. Prayer can change the atmosphere, prayer can change the cultural climate, and prayer can change the atmospheric conditions.

One of the goals of the church collectively, is to control the moral and spiritual atmosphere in our communities and in our cities. Individually, as believers, we would personally like to control the atmosphere in our homes.

We need not just be disgusted and concerned when we see destructive events we need to pray. What would it be like if we exercised the power to control the elements and declare in the face of those destined to lead us down a road to destruction and immorality that as Elijah said to King Ahab, *"As the LORD God of Israel liveth, before whom I stand, there shall not be dew nor rain these years, but according to my word"* 1 Kings 17:1 (KJV). We would have the attention of those in positions of leadership. As believers, we have both the comfort and the cure.

****

A winter drought threatened the crop in a village of Crete. The priest told his flock: "There isn't anything that will save us, except a special litany, meaning a spiritual confession by the body at large, for rain. Go to your homes, fast during the week, believe, and come on Sunday for the litany of rain." The villagers heard him, fasted during the week, and went to the church on Sunday morning, but as soon as the priest saw them, he was furious. He said, "Go away; I will not do the litany. You do not believe." "But Father," they protested, "we fasted and we believe." "Believe? And where are your umbrellas?"

When we pray we must believe that God is going to do something. As the priest says, we must have a sense of expectancy. We must pray with confidence, because we have a good God and His promise is sure, because His Word says so. We hold on to His promises and pray.

As James nears the close of his letter to the church, we reflect that he has laid out through this whole letter some serious and real challenges to the church, some real life evils, and sins to fight against.

James started his letter telling the church to ask God for wisdom and now he closes the letter with a wonderful word of encouragement. That is the power of prayer in every situation available to every Christian not to super-saints but to every one of like passions like an Elijah.

If the church is ever going to make a difference in our world, if we are going to change the atmosphere in our city, our community, our church, and in our homes:

- It isn't going to be only through our fantastic programs, and our large missionary budgets

- It isn't going to be by our great education or attracting the most skilled orators
- It isn't going to be because we are willing to serve

It is going to be nothing less than us as a body walking daily in the power of God. Walking daily in the power of prayer; knowing that we are treading in waters that we cannot survive in, or on our own.[25]. God acts in response to our prayers.

We need to pray. Andrew Murray writes, "God's giving is inseparably connected with our asking. . . . Only by intercession can that power be brought down from heaven which will enable the Church to conquer the world." We have the assurance of answered prayer.

Jesus tells us, *"And whatever things you ask in prayer, believing, you will receive"* (Matt 21:22).

The Apostles John affirms this, *"Now this is the confidence that we have in Him, that if we ask anything according to His will, He hears us. And if we know that He hears us, whatever we ask, we know that we have the petitions that we have asked of Him"* (1 John 5:14-15).

That puts a lot of responsibility upon our shoulders. This responsibility is a privilege. God is not powerless to do anything, but He has given us the great responsibility to bring about a change in our world today through prayer. People's lives are changed because of prayer. We have the ability to control the atmosphere.

Prayer changes things, because God acts in response to our prayer. Do you want to see a change in your life, in your family, in your friends' lives? We have to pray.

REFLECTIONS AND MEDITATIONS

1. How confident are you in sharing your prayer requests believing that they will be heard?

---

25 http://www.sermoncentral.com/sermons/Experiencing the Power of Prayer, Stephan Brown

2. Can you recall a specific incident in your life where you knew it was the response to prayer?
3. In light of the many natural disasters we regularly observe, can we believe that prayer really can make a difference?

CHAPTER 15

"PURSUING WANDERERS

James 5:19-20

> Our lives are to be dedicated in service to reconciling people to God and to one another.
>
> *Brethren, if anyone among you wanders from the truth, and someone turns him back, let him know that he who turns a sinner from the error of his way will save a soul from death and cover a multitude of sins. (James 5:19-20)*

These two verses bring us to the end of the book of James. In our study of the book of James, we have found his five-chapter letter filled with multitudes of different instructions and exhortations to try to get brethren to live faithfully. He has spoken in his letter about many problems: sinful speech, disobedience, unconcern about others, worldliness, quarreling, arrogance, and prayerlessness. Now he encourages every believer to take the initiative in bringing any who have wandered *'from the truth'* in any of these areas back into fellowship with God and the community.

In the last chapter, James, using the example of Elijah, called us to pray believing that through prayer we could control the atmosphere, meaning the situation of those who are sick: weak, weary, and physically ill. Here James speaks of those who have lost their way as being the "sick ones" of the church family. Their infirmity is that they have wandered away. We are called to pursue them and reconcile them to God.

HOW DOES ONE WANDER FROM THE TRUTH?

> *"Brethren, if anyone among you wanders from the truth . . ."* (vs. 19a)

James uses the word "*brethren*" 15 times in the five chapters. He has and is referring to those who are members of the church, both males and females, who have accepted the gospel and were saved of their past sins. This is a message for you and for me.

James says "*if,*" which is a conditional term that says, 'just in case.' It is like a flashing yellow light, which says, "Caution," "beware," there is danger ahead.

When we speak of someone wandering, it is often reflective of children, who become infatuated or curious about what they see. The spirit of exploration and a desire to experience something new, to touch or sense something beyond their present reality, often draws them away for the security of their parents. Those of us who are parents know the mixed feeling of fear and anger of having a child wander off.

That is also true of adults; we often refer to it as "wanderlust" defined as; *A strong, innate desire to rove or travel about.* Wanderlust can lead to a compromise of the truth of the Word of God. Marital partners often wander from the fidelity of their marriage, lusting for something new, exciting and different, lusting for what seems to be greener on the other side of the fence, so to speak. The truth about the marital relationship is that when two people marry they become one. Any side relationship breaks the bond of oneness. The oneness becomes a threesome.

Older singles and young people do the same thinking that they are missing something, or expecting that the relationship they will have with that man or woman, that boy or girl will give them the sense of wholeness they feel is missing in their lives. The truth about those who engage in premarital sexual activity is that they become one with that person, and successive engagement with different partners, results in giving so much away that they find themselves empty of who they are. They have given so much of themselves away that they lose sight of who they are and therefore have little or no self-esteem.

The inclination to wander towards evil, towards compromise, to adopting that which is contrary to the Word of God is not typically one overt act. It is something that gradually occurs over time. It begins in a thought, moves to more lustful consideration, then to planning how it might be accomplished, and then ultimately to sin.

Sin is serious business in the life of a believer. It harms our spirit, cripples our walk with God, and it hinders the Holy Spirit's work in our life. In Joshua 7:20-21, we are told of Achan's sin. Therein, he expressed the progressive path to his downfall. He said, *"Indeed I have sinned against the Lord God of Israel, and this is what I have done: "When I saw among the spoils a beautiful Babylonian garment, two hundred shekels of silver, and a wedge of gold weighing fifty shekels, I coveted them and took them. And there they are, hidden in the earth in the midst of my tent, with the silver under it."* It was a progressive work: he saw, desired, and committed the theft.

James declares in 1:13-15 that succumbing to temptation is no one's fault but our own. *"Let no one say when he is tempted, "I am tempted by God"; for God cannot be tempted by evil, nor does He Himself tempt anyone. But each one is tempted when he is drawn away by his own desires and enticed. Then, when desire has conceived, it gives birth to sin; and sin, when it is full-grown, brings forth death.* Sin is a progressive work: it is visual desire, physical satisfaction, gives birth to sin, and results in destruction.

The worldly enticements are designed to draw us away from the truth. There is in each of us a desire for the satisfaction of the desires and needs of self. This is what got Eve into trouble in the first place.

This is why it is so important to attend church regularly, to read our bible, to stay prayed up, because the enticements of the world are continually calling our flesh away from the truth. However, Proverbs 5:14 tells us that we can wander from the truth even when we regularly attend church. *"How I have hated instruction, and my heart despised correction! I have not obeyed the voice of my teachers, nor inclined my ear to those who instructed me! I was on the verge of total ruin, in the midst of the assembly and congregation."*

The devil continually brings before us that which draws us away. Even the apostle Paul acknowledged the danger and his tendency to give into them. In Romans 7:19 (KJV) he declares, *"For the good that I would I do not: but the evil which I would not, that I do."*

Like sheep, we can become so consumed in eating of the world's food that we lose sight of the fact that we are eating our way towards the cliff of destruction. We must look up from time to time and evaluate where we are before we fall over the edge of destruction.

WE ARE CALLED TO BE THAT SOMEONE.

". . . and someone turns him back" (vs. 19b)

The job of a shepherd is to keep his sheep from wandering off. The job of a parent is to keep an eye on children and call them back when they get too far away. The responsibility that we have towards each other is to hold each other accountable.

We often get this matter of accountability and judging confused. There are those who say we ought not to judge, and in the proper context there is good biblical foundation for that. However, we often misunderstand the context and purpose for which that statement is made. It is correct that we ought not to judge a person's character. We ought not to use words like worthless, no good, will never be nothin', stupid, and the like speaking of God's creation. We are not called to make those kinds of assessments. That ought to be left up to God. However, we are called to hold each other accountable-not by any standard-but according to the Word of God. Each of us has a responsibility to help each other to live up to what we claim to be. If we claim to be children of God, each of us has a responsibility to tell each other when our conduct is unbecoming of the claim.

When we see someone, a brother, or sister in Christ, wandering away from the truth, we have a responsibility to inform them of danger. A responsibility to call to their attention what good Christian conduct looks like. We have a responsibility to snatch them for the fangs of the devil, from the ravages of sin, from off the road of compromise.

The legal system deals with the criminal in terms of condemnation and punishment; the church, the believer must see him or her as a wandering brother or sister who must be redeemed.

Some of us think it is the preacher's job. Some of us think we do not know enough to correct someone straying from the truth. However, God has placed in each of us natural level of conscience. Unless we have become totally blinded by sin, we sense and know what is right and wrong.

- You don't have to be a theologian to see that drinking and drugging is contrary to the spirit of good health
- You don't have to be a theologian to know that sex outside of marriage will destroy the relationship with your husband or wife, result in pregnancy, possibility acquiring an STD, and ruin your reputation

Even unbelievers are aware of those dangers and can perceive the destructive elements. The difference is that they have no mandate to speak in God's name to snatch back a brother or sister from destruction. However, we are called to be that someone! If we see one of our spiritual family, wandering away from the truth it is not just the job of the church leaders to go after them but also the job of all.

If we see our neighbors two year old walking down the street, we would go get them, we would not say that is not my job especially if we saw them heading into a busy dangerous street. The word *someone* indicates that we are all responsible to do what we can. To bring them back means to help bring them to repentance.

Everyone is precious and valuable in the family of God. Not only are we to love one another but we are to learn from one another because we help one another.

WHOSE BLESSING IS IT?

> "... *let him know that he who turns a sinner from the error of his way will save a soul from death and cover a multitude of sins.* (vs. 20)

James is talking about converting one who has already become a member of the church, a believer. James is referring to bringing a backslider back from their wanderings and motivating him or her to turn from the error of their way.

We are called to wonder whose soul and whose sin is James speaking of here. Is he speaking of the one who calls someone back to the truth? On the other hand, is he speaking of the one who wandered and is brought back? The Greek is completely ambiguous at this point, allowing either phrase to be applied to the one who has sinned or the one who has converted the sinner.

However, the soul, which has been saved from death, is almost certainly the soul of the one who has sinned, but it is more difficult to know whether the sins, which are covered, are the sinner's the converter's, or both.

First Peter 4:8 would seem to support that reconciling another to God carries a personal blessing to the reconciler, *"And above all things have fervent love for one another, for "love will cover a multitude of sins."*

Can a person who performs the good work of converting an erring soul by this act cover a multitude of his own sins? According to strict "evangelical" teaching, good works, though ever so numerous, can never atone for sins, though they be ever so few.

However, I think we can safely say to turn a sinner from error confers a double benefit; it helps not only the "converted" soul but the "converting" soul as well.[26]

Whosever sins are covered, clearly God has given to us the ministry of reconciliation. It is our duty, responsibility, and expression of God's love and purpose in Christ for us to reconcile others to Christ. Responsibility for this ministry of reconciliation is laid upon the ordinary Christian, not upon the minister or priest. Each church member is expected to accept responsibility for every other church member. Each member of the congregation is responsible for the welfare of every other member of the congregation. We must accept responsibility to be sensitive to the signs of straying and to hold one another accountable for continuing to walk in the way of the Master.

****

When evangelist D. L. Moody was conducting evangelistic meetings, he frequently faced hecklers who strongly disagreed with him. In the final service of one campaign, an usher handed the famous preacher a note as he entered the auditorium. It was actually from an atheist who had been giving Mr. Moody a great deal of trouble. The evangelist, however, thought that it was an announcement, so he quieted the large audience and prepared to read it. Opening the folded piece of paper he found scrawled in large print only one word: "Fool" The colorful preacher was equal to the occasion. Said Moody, "I have just been handed a memo which contains the single word—'Fool.' This is most unusual. I've often heard of those who have written letters and forgotten to sign their names, but this is the first time I've ever heard of anyone who signed his name and then forgot to write the letter." Taking advantage of the unique situation, Moody promptly changed his

---

26 George Arthur Buttrick, *The Interpreter's Bible, Vol. 12-James*, (New York, NY: Abingdon, 1957), 73

sermon text to Psalm 14:1: "The fool says in his heart, 'There is no God'" [27]

Our expectation ought to be that we will have criticism from those who are unbelievers. However, Christians should be in the business of helping one another, bearing one another's burdens. Nevertheless, some Christians are more critical than they are caring! They are more of a hindrance than a help! Let us not get confused about the spiritual task of restoring a wandering soul with telling people how bad they have been.

- No sheep ever decided to get lost; but sheep do nevertheless become lost
- No Christian ever came into the Faith with a determination to stray; but Christians do stray
- No child of God ever began to follow the Savior with the desire to turn aside after false teachers; but children of the Living God are led astray by false teachers

Believers can and do deceive themselves, straying into error and deserting the path of righteousness.

Today we who have been reconciled to God serve as Christ's ambassadors, in order to bring others to Christ who paid their death penalty that they may be reconciled to God, restored to a peaceful relationship with God. Christ did it with his death. We do it with our lives. We do it when we tell of his death and how it brings us from sin into salvation. Second Corinthians 5:18-20 declares, *Now all things are of God, who has reconciled us to Himself through Jesus Christ, and has given us the ministry of reconciliation, that is, that God was in Christ reconciling the world to Himself, not imputing their trespasses to them, and has committed to us the word of reconciliation. Now then, we are ambassadors for Christ, as though God were pleading through us: we implore you on Christ's behalf, be reconciled to God.*

---

[27] http://www.sermoncentral.com/Illustrations/When Evangelist D. L. Moody Was Conducting ...

All Christians have been called to the ministry of reconciliation. Our lives are to be dedicated in service to reconciling people to God and to one another. To do so we must be willing to invest ourselves in the lives of others. How do we do that?

1. Be aware there is a problem
2. Pray for the one who has wandered, do not despise or condemn them
3. Pray for yourself so that your heart is right in trying to help
4. Make personal contact. If you are not a part of their life, you cannot help
5. Be ready to share with them the truth in love
6. Be a living example of the truth in your own life
7. Encourage them to come back home

REFLECTIONS AND MEDITATIONS

1. Do you recognize the path that leads to sin and guard your thoughts and actions against it?
2. Have you allowed God to be crowded out of your life and wandered towards the ways of the world?
3. Do you acknowledge your responsibility to speak a word of correction to those who are going astray

Compact discs of these messages are available.

William is available for preaching, workshops, conferences, and other ministry events.

You may learn more about William Golson by visiting: HYPERLINK "http://www.truelightonline.org" www.truelightonline.org
William may be personally contacted by email: HYPERLINK "mailto:revgolson@aol.com" revgolson@aol.com
Or:
William T. Golson, Jr.
P.O. Box 39003
Denver CO 80239-0003

Other Publications by the Author:
On the Matter of Relationships (Xulon Press)
Adjusting Your Copy Quality: Becoming Who the Word Says You Are (Xulon Press)
Good Advice From A Player (Trafford Publishing)
Facing Giants: Don't Let Giants Cause You A Faith Failure (Xulon Press)

Printed in the United States
By Bookmasters